Before Anything Else, Validate

The Missing Link in Healing, Leadership, Relationships, and Personal Growth

By Mardoche Sidor, M.D., Karen Dubin, Ph.D., LCSW, and SWEET Institute

SWEET Institute Publishing
Transformational Books for a Transformational World

Copyright © 2025 by the SWEET Institute
All rights reserved.

No part of this book may be reproduced, stored in a retrieval system, or transmitted in any form or by any means — electronic, mechanical, photocopying, recording, or otherwise — without the prior written permission of the publisher, except in the case of brief quotations embodied in critical articles or reviews.

Published by:
SWEET Institute Publishing
New York, NY
WWW.SWEETInstitutePublishing.com

First Edition
Printed in the United States of America

ISBN (Paperback): 978-1-968105-09-9

Library of Congress Control Number: 2025942692

Cover Design by SWEET Institute Publishing
Interior Design and Layout by SWEET Institute Publishing
For bulk orders, permissions, or media inquiries, please contact:
contact@sweetinstitute.com

Unless otherwise noted, all stories and case examples in this book are either fictionalized or used with permission, and identifying details have been changed to protect the privacy of individuals.

SWEET Institute Publishing
Transformational Books for a Transformational World

Dedication

To every child who ever wondered,
"Am I good enough?"
To every adult who still does.

To the mother, the father, the teacher, the leader—
who showed us, in a single glance or word,
that we mattered.

To the brave souls who go without it,
and the even braver ones who learn to give it to themselves.

And to the world we are building—
where before anything else,
we validate.

Other Books by Mardoche Sidor, M.D; Karen Dubin, PhD, LCSW; with the SWEET Institute

- Journey to Empowerment
- Discovering Your Worth: Everything You Need to Feel Fulfilled
- The Power of Faith: A Harvard-Trained Psychiatrist Speaking on Faith
- The Psychotherapy Certificate Course: The Clinician and Coach Manual (Books 1–3)
- The Anxiety Course: The Workbook
- What's Missing
- NLP for Clinicians
- 50 SWEET Poems: Reflections on life, love and self
- The Power of Belief: How Ideas Shape Leaders, Nations and the Future
- The Courage to Care: Stories of Healing, Hope, and the Power of Social Work: Told by Over 50 SWEET Institute Social Workers
- Transforming Team Relationships from the Inside Out: The SWEET Healing Circle for Agencies: Redefining Accountability, Collaboration, and Culture
- Remembering: The Journey Back to the Pre-Conditioned Self
- The Clinician's Mirror: A Story of Projection, Self-Awareness, and Transformation for Clinicians
- The Secret Is in Remembering: Why We Suffer, Why We Forget, and How to Return to Who We Are
- It's All Perfect: What If Nothing in Your Life Was a Mistake?
- Because of Us: Why Outcomes Change When We Do
- Rewriting the Script: The Power of Transforming Inner Dialogue in Oppressed Communities

Table of Contents

Foreword	7
Preface	10
Introduction	12
Why This Book	14
What This Book Is About	15
How to Read This Book	16
How This Book Works	17
Acknowledgments	20
Chapter 1: What We All Crave – The Universal Need for Validation	22
Chapter 2: How It All Begins – Childhood, Conditioning, and Reinforcement	29
Chapter 3: The External Chase – Friends, Partners, Society, and the World	35
Chapter 3: The External Chase – Friends, Partners, Society, and the World	38
Chapter 4: Validation's Power – From Art to Atrocity	41
Chapter 5: When It Stops Working – The Crisis of Misplaced Worth	48
Chapter 6: Turning Inward – Discovering the Source Within	55
Chapter 7: The Practice of Self-Validation – Tools for Everyday Life	63
Chapter 8: Learning to Listen – Inner Voice, Inner Child, Inner Truth	70
Chapter 8: Learning to Listen – Inner Voice, Inner Child, Inner Truth	73

Chapter 9: Mirror Work, Journaling, and the Neuroscience of Worth	75
Chapter 10: Rewiring the Brain – How Internal Validation Reshapes Us	82
Chapter 11: Validating Others – Every Interaction as an Opportunity	87
Chapter 12: Modeling Validation – At Work, Home, and in Leadership	93
Chapter 13: Validation in Therapy, Teaching, Parenting, and Healing	99
Chapter 13: Validation in Therapy, Teaching, Parenting, and Healing	103
Chapter 14: The Art of Collective Validation – Cultures of Inclusion	106
Chapter 14: The Art of Collective Validation – Cultures of Inclusion	109
Chapter 15: The Reciprocity Principle – Giving and Receiving in Balance	113

Epilogue: You Were Always Enough	**120**
Conclusion: The New Way Forward	**121**
Invitation to the Reader	**123**
Final Acknowledgments	**125**
Reader Integration Toolkit	**126**
Appendices and Tools	**129**
Scientific Reference List	**132**
Recommended Reading	**134**
More from SWEET Institute Publishing	**136**
About the Authors	138

Foreword
By Lydia Watling, LMSW

Social Worker | ACT Team Practitioner | SWEET Institute Postgraduate

Before I learned the science of validation, I felt its absence. I can remember a day during childhood when I was in floods of tears begging my mother "please tell me it's okay to be angry!" The absence of validation from an early start was essentially normal for me and it wasn't without its effects. my norm became turning outward to search the faces of others hoping they'd give me a sign that whatever I was doing or saying was acceptable. I constantly scanned the outside waiting for others approval that being myself was good enough. It's a very closed in (and not fun!) way to live!

I saw the absence not only in my own life but in the systems in New York and in the families I serve across the Cayman Islands.

I heard it in the silence of children who had stopped trying to explain themselves. The ones who appeared stone cold from years of being unseen and unheard; the ones who lacked an adult to reflect back to them that they're essentially good just as they are.

I felt it in the disconnect between systems that meant well—and the people those systems were supposed to serve- where jumping to fix perceived problems without first seeking to understand and make sense of another's world was just the way things were done.

And I recognized it in myself: in the parts of me that still waited for someone else to say, "You are enough."

That's why this book matters. That's why I said yes when I was asked to write this foreword.

Before Anything Else, Validate is not just a title—it's a principle, a practice, and a quiet revolution. It names the one thing that all healing has in common: the need to be seen.

Through my work on ACT Teams at CASES, in NYC, in my work in the Caribbean, and as a dedicated postgraduate student clinician of the SWEET Institute, I've witnessed the difference validation makes—not in theory, but in lived experience. I've learned that people don't change because we diagnose them, or direct them, or discipline them. They change because someone paused long enough to say, "What's happening in you makes sense. Let's start there."

And I've watched my own life begin to change when I applied the same pause to myself.

This book gives language to what so many of us feel but don't know how to name. It combines the relational wisdom of clinical practice with the inner work of becoming a more whole human being. It's science-based, story-driven, and spiritually honest. And most of all, it's doable. You won't be left alone with a bunch of knowledge and no way to apply it.

Karen and Mardoche don't just talk about validation. They model it—through every word, every prompt, every dialogue in this book. They've taught me (and thousands of other SWEET clinicians around the world) that experiential learning and implementation are the bridge between knowing and becoming. We need to practice with ourselves first, to grasp wholeheartedly the essence of the experience, and do it again and again so that when we work with others we can give to them all we have given to ourselves. In this book, they hand you the tools to build that bridge — chapter by chapter, breath by breath, moment by moment.

If you work with people, live with people, lead people — or if you're just trying to be more fully yourself — this book is your companion. It will teach you to validate without losing boundaries, to listen without fixing, and to be present without pretense.

It will also remind you, again and again, that validation is not something you wait for. It's something you practice.

And that practice, when done with intention, becomes your gift to the world.

May this book awaken your courage, deepen your empathy, and ignite your transformation.

Because before anything else...

You deserve to be seen.

Lydia Watling, LMSW
Social Worker
Former ACT Team Practitioner at CASES, NYC
Postgraduate and Practitioner of the SWEET Method

Preface

By Mardoche Sidor, MD

In almost two decades of psychiatric practice, I have seen more suffering born from invalidation than from any diagnosis, symptom, or circumstance. A person can live through trauma, loss, injustice, and pain; but when their reality is dismissed, their voice silenced, or their worth denied, something deeper breaks. That's why this book, *Before Anything Else, Validate*, is more than timely, it's essential.

Validation is often misunderstood. It's mistaken for agreement, praise, or indulgence. But at its core, validation is the recognition of experience. It's saying: I see you, I hear you, you make sense. These nine words, when genuine, can reroute a lifetime of self-doubt.

Through this book, we have taken what clinicians know from research, what leaders learn through failure, what parents discover through trial and error, and what all of us, at our most honest, yearn for. And we've turned it into a deeply readable, scientifically grounded, and emotionally resonant guide.

We hope you will find yourself in these pages; and more importantly, you will find the people you serve, love, teach, supervise, or try to understand. Whether you're a psychiatrist, a social worker, a parent, or a CEO, this book will give you the tools to create connection where there was disconnection, safety where there was shame, and growth where there was stagnation.

In a time when division is easy and understanding feels rare, this book is an invitation to something deeper. To validate is to begin again. It is the first act of healing, the first step in leadership, the first expression of love.

May this book reach you as it has reached me, while writing it— with clarity, urgency, and compassion.

Mardoche, MD
Quadruple Board Certified Psychiatrist

Introduction

By Karen Dubin, PhD, LCSW

There are books that inform. There are books that inspire. And then there are rare books that do both while reshaping the very language we use to understand ourselves and others. *Before Anything Else, Validate* is that kind of book.

As a social worker, educator, supervisor, and advocate, I've had the privilege of witnessing the evolution of our understanding of mental health and human behavior. And while our field has made significant strides in diagnostics, treatment, and neurobiological research, we often overlook the fundamental emotional truths that determine when healing begins. Validation is one of those truths. This book returns us to that foundation, beautifully, powerfully, and unapologetically.

What we hope we have done here is more than write a book. We hope we have issued a call: to clinicians, to educators, to leaders, to parents, to all of us — A call to recognize that before we offer insight, intervention, or advice, we are to first offer presence, acknowledgment, and respect for one's lived experience.

Drawing from clinical science, developmental psychology, behavioral theory, and timeless human wisdom, this book walks the reader through the universal longing to be seen and the life-altering power of being validated. It makes a strong, evidence-based case for why validation isn't optional. It's the cornerstone of mental health, the driver of emotional development, and the key to relational success.

You will learn the neuroscience behind validation. You'll explore the psychology of why it matters so much. You'll reflect on your own life, your own wounds, and your own capacity to show up differently. And perhaps most meaningfully, you'll gain practical tools to help others feel heard, whether you're in an exam room, a boardroom, a classroom, or a living room.

We are, each of us, shaped by the messages we receive about our worth. And far too often, those messages come from silence, dismissal, and misunderstanding. *Before Anything Else, Validate* shows us how to change that—one conversation at a time.

I am honored to introduce this work to you. May it serve as a guide, a mirror, and a call to action.

Karen Dubin, PhD, LCSW

COO, SWEET Institute

Why This Book

Because we've all lived with the question: "Am I enough?"

Because we live in a world where people are judged before they are heard, advised before they are understood, and corrected before they are acknowledged.

Because the child who never felt validated grows into the adult who still seeks it. And because this cycle repeats, generation after generation, unless we do something radically different.

Because validation is not soft, it is strong. It is the backbone of effective therapy, transformational leadership, secure attachment, and authentic self-worth.

Because we are ready to stop looking outside for approval, and instead start creating a world where everyone knows they matter, starting with ourselves.

Because before anything else, we ought to validate.

What This Book Is About

This book is a journey through psychology, relationships, leadership, healing, and personal transformation. It reveals how validation shapes our brains, drives our behaviors, and determines the quality of our connections.

You'll discover:

- Why validation is the foundation of human development
- How we seek it, consciously and unconsciously, from childhood onward
- The neuroscience of validation and why it's so powerful
- The dangers of external-only validation
- How to cultivate self-validation as a practice
- How to validate others, genuinely and effectively
- How validation can change families, workplaces, communities, and the world

It's part clinical, part spiritual, part practical, and entirely human.

How to Read This Book

This book is designed to be read, reflected on, and lived.

Each chapter blends engaging dialogue, scientific insights, and practical tools. You'll find:

- Reflections and prompts to deepen your self-awareness
- Exercises and practices to try in real life
- Infographics and tables to clarify key concepts
- Case examples from individuals across roles and backgrounds
- Scientific citations to ground the wisdom in research

You can read straight through or skip to chapters that call to you. Use the exercises in your practice, your parenting, or your leadership. Share it with your team, your clients, your partner, or yourself.

Let this be more than a book. Let it be a mirror, a manual, and a movement.

How This Book Works

This is not just a book to read. It's a book to experience.

You'll find stories, science, and strategies woven together in a way that speaks to the mind, the heart, and the body. This book is designed not only to inform you—but to transform you.

Here's how:

1. Conversational Structure

Each chapter is written in the form of a dialogue between you, the Reader, and two guides—Dr. Sidor and Dr. Dubin. This style invites you into intimate, reflective, and often surprising conversations that mirror the therapeutic and transformational process of learning to validate yourself and others.

2. Scientific Integration

Every concept is backed by peer-reviewed scientific research. From neurobiology to developmental psychology, you'll see validation through the lens of rigorous evidence and human truth. Each chapter concludes with a list of scientific references.

3. Visual Learning Tools

Infographics, charts, diagrams, and tables appear throughout the book (and in the companion toolkit) to make complex ideas visual and accessible. These tools are designed to reinforce understanding and support different learning styles.

4. Reflections and Prompts

At the end of each chapter, you'll find carefully crafted reflection questions. These are not rhetorical. Pause, write, speak, and let them land. These prompts help move you from passive reading to active integration.

5. Practical Exercises

Each chapter also contains real-world practices — from mirror work and journal prompts to validation scripts and communication tools. These are meant to be used, repeated, adapted, and embodied. Information becomes transformation only when practiced.

6. Four Levels of Transformation

This book is built on a layered model:

- Conscious – the level of thought and awareness
- Preconscious – the habits and patterns just beneath the surface
- Unconscious – the deeper drivers of emotion, identity, and defense
- Existential – the level of meaning, presence, and purpose

Every chapter speaks to all four, helping you move from head to heart to action to truth.

7. Companion Toolkit

You'll find a full downloadable toolkit that includes:

- Printable worksheets
- Visuals for each chapter
- Practice trackers
- Group and leadership tools

This makes the work portable, teachable, and shareable.

Acknowledgments

This book was written in conversation with the world.

To every person who has ever asked, "Do I matter?" — this is for you.

We begin by thanking the people we serve, work alongside, learn from, and walk with daily. You've shown us what validation looks like when it's absent, and what it becomes when it's offered with truth and compassion. Your stories shaped every page of this book.

To the residents, clients, patients, students, and community members who have allowed us to bear witness to your pain and your power — you have been our greatest teachers.

To the team and community at the SWEET Institute: your commitment to truth, healing, and integrity is the heartbeat of everything we do. Thank you for modeling the very principles we write about — every day, in every encounter.

To the clinicians, educators, and leaders who practice presence in a world of pressure: thank you for choosing to validate before you intervene, for listening before you lead, for being brave enough to care.

To the researchers and pioneers who have illuminated the science of validation — from Marsha Linehan to Kristin Neff, Dan Siegel to Stephen Porges — your work gave this book its backbone.

To our families: for the early lessons—both the ones we're healing from and the ones we now carry forward with love. Your influence is in our process, our pauses, and our desire to do better.

To our readers: thank you for holding this book in your hands. That act alone is a declaration—one that says the way we speak to ourselves and each other matters. May this book be a mirror, a tool, and a companion on your journey.

And finally, to every part of ourselves that once longed to be seen:

We see you now.

With respect, love, and deep gratitude,

Mardoche Sidor, M.D.
Karen Dubin, Ph.D., LCSW
and SWEET Institute

Chapter 1: What We All Crave – The Universal Need for Validation

Scene: A sunlit therapy office. Three voices — Dr. Sidor (psychiatrist), Dr. Dubin (social worker), and a curious Reader — begin a conversation that echoes through every life.

Reader:

Why do we need validation so much? Why does it matter, even when we're "grown up" and supposedly independent?

Dr. Sidor:

That's the question at the heart of every session I've ever held. Every single one of us — regardless of age, culture, profession — wants to know: Am I seen? Do I matter? It's not weakness. It's human nature.

Dr. Dubin:

It starts before we can even speak. Infants, moments after birth, search for their caregiver's face. The way a mother gazes back, the warmth in a father's voice — these are our first lessons in belonging. Neurologically, these moments wire our brains for connection.

Research shows that parental responsiveness and attunement shape a child's developing brain, impacting emotional regulation and even immune health (Feldman, 2015; Schore, 2012).

Reader:

But aren't we supposed to "grow out of it"? Isn't needing validation a sign of insecurity?

Dr. Sidor:

It's a myth. Sure, as adults, we learn to survive without external approval, but at a cost. People who never felt validated as children often struggle with self-worth, confidence, or boundaries later on. The truth? Needing to be seen is as vital as needing air.

Dr. Dubin:

Think of it this way: validation is the emotional oxygen of life. And just like oxygen, we notice its absence much more than its presence.

Reader:

So, what does validation really mean? Is it praise? Agreement? Approval?

Dr. Sidor:

Great question. Validation isn't about flattery or permissiveness. It's about reflecting back someone's reality. "I see how hard this is for you." "Your feelings make sense." It's the difference between feeling invisible and feeling real.

Dr. Dubin:

And it's everywhere. In childhood, we seek it from parents and teachers. In adolescence, from peers. As adults, from partners, bosses, friends, and even strangers. Social media, for better or worse, has become a global validation marketplace.

Reader:

But if everyone's looking for validation, what happens when we don't get it?

Dr. Sidor:

We adapt – sometimes in healthy ways, sometimes not. We might try harder to please, or withdraw, or rebel. In extreme cases, the lack of validation is linked to depression, anxiety, self-harm, even aggression (Linehan, 1993; Baumeister & Leary, 1995).

Dr. Dubin:

Or we start looking for it anywhere we can – chasing achievement, approval, "likes," even unhealthy relationships. We become experts at reading the faces of others, asking without words: Do I matter to you?

Reader:

It sounds exhausting.

Dr. Sidor:

It is. But here's the truth that can change everything - Validation isn't just something to get from others. It's something we can learn to give ourselves – and, in doing so, finally breathe free.

Reflections and Prompts

- Who are the people whose validation you still crave?
- When did you first realize you needed to feel "seen"?
- Recall a moment you felt deeply validated. What made it so powerful?
- What are the ways you seek validation – directly or indirectly?

Practical Exercise

Validation Journal:

For one week, write down each time you notice yourself seeking validation – from anyone (family, friends, strangers, social media). Notice the patterns. No judgment, just observation.

Chapter 1: The Power of Validation

Infographic: The Life Cycle of Validation

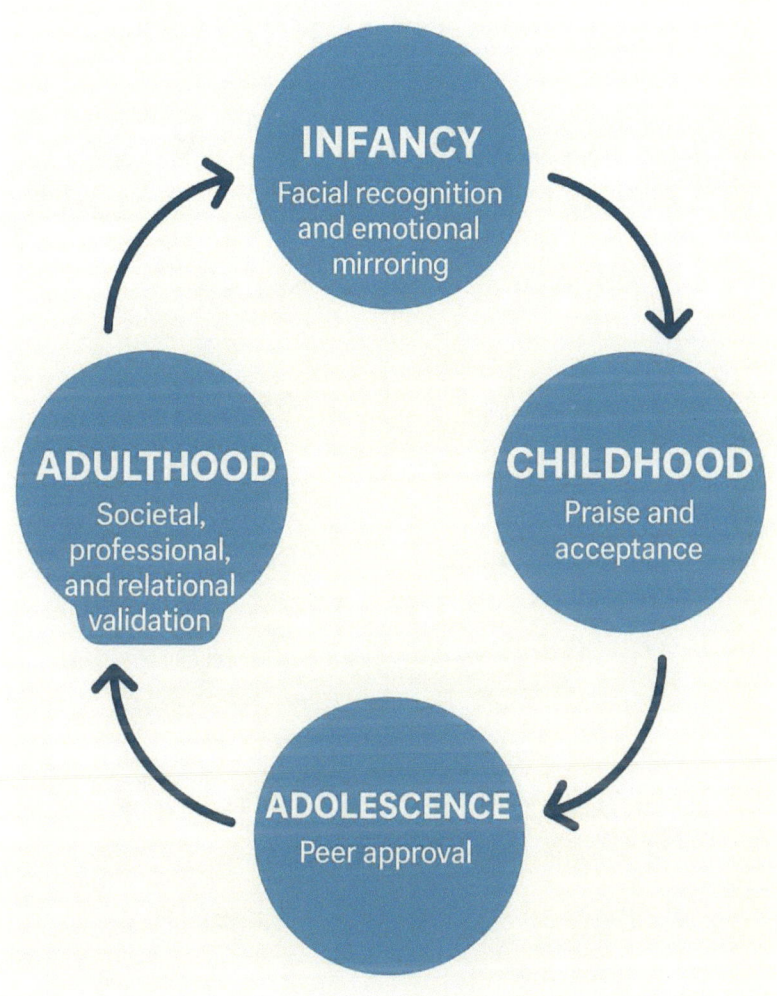

Each stage builds internal narratives of self-worth.

Table: Healthy vs. Unhealthy Sources of Validation

Healthy vs. Unhealthy Sources of Validation

Healthy	Unhealthy
Self Worth	Appearance
Loved Ones	Social Media
Healthy Relationships	Codependent Relationships
Constructive Feedback	Approval Seeking
Personal Values	Perfectionism
Achievement	Superiority

Flow Chart: What Happens When Validation Is Missing?

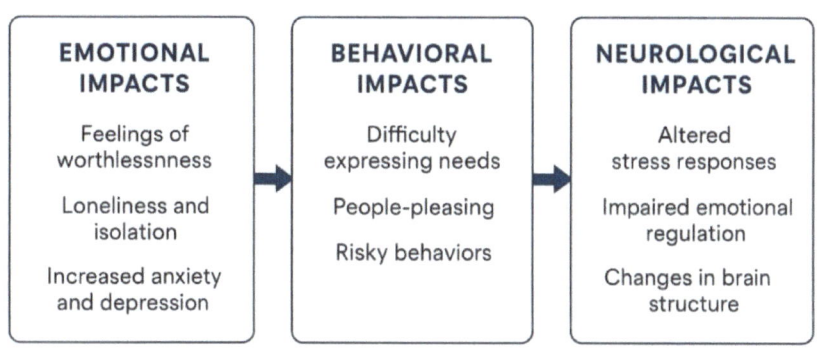

Infographic: The Validation-Seeking Loop

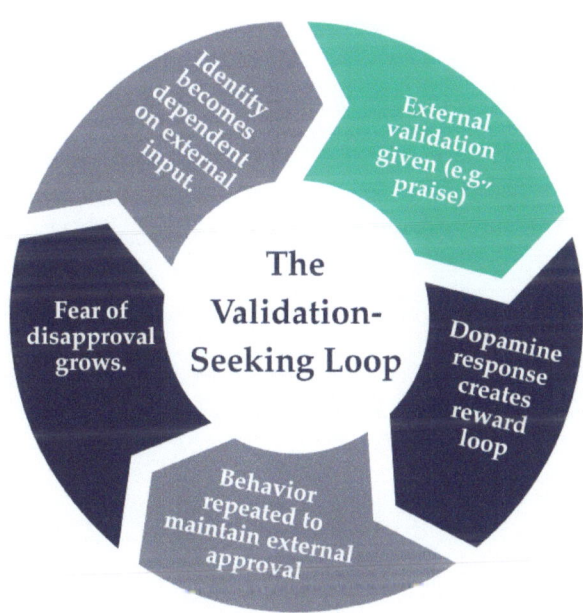

Scientific References

- Baumeister, R. F., & Leary, M. R. (1995). The need to belong: Desire for interpersonal attachments as a fundamental human motivation. Psychological Bulletin, 117(3), 497-529.
- Feldman, R. (2015). Sensitive periods in human social development: New insights from research on oxytocin, attachment, and synchrony. Developmental Psychopathology, 27(2), 369-395.
- Linehan, M. M. (1993). Cognitive-Behavioral Treatment of Borderline Personality Disorder. New York: Guilford Press.
- Schore, A. N. (2012). The science of the art of psychotherapy. New York: Norton.

Chapter 2: How It All Begins – Childhood, Conditioning, and Reinforcement

Scene: A quiet park bench. Dr. Sidor, Dr. Dubin, and the Reader sit watching children play. A conversation unfolds about the first time we ever looked for validation.

Reader:

They look so free – those kids running around. Do they even know they're being shaped?

Dr. Dubin:

Not consciously. But everything happening here – the glances, reactions, praise, scolding, silence – it's shaping their inner world. These children are learning what gets them love, attention, and acceptance. They're building what psychologists call operant associations – learning what's reinforced and what's rejected.

Dr. Sidor:

A baby babbles, then looks at her caregiver. If they smile or clap, she babbles more. If they look away or frown, she might stop. This is the beginning of contingent learning – and at its heart is validation.

Reader:

So, we're literally wired to look outward first?

Dr. Sidor:

Exactly. Developmental psychology and attachment theory both confirm it: We learn who we are by how others reflect us back to ourselves. That's why early experiences of validation – or invalidation – leave such a lasting mark.

Studies by Mary Ainsworth, John Bowlby, and more recently Dan Siegel show how attuned caregiving builds secure attachment and healthy emotional regulation.

Dr. Dubin:

It's not just about what's said. It's about tone, timing, presence. The child who cries and is met with, "You're too sensitive," begins to question her emotions. The child who is told, "Big boys don't cry," learns to suppress his vulnerability. These messages become internalized scripts.

Reader:

So, what starts as a need for external feedback becomes a lifelong inner voice?

Dr. Sidor:

Exactly. A voice that says, "You're not enough unless you achieve," or "Your feelings aren't valid," or "Love is something you have to earn." And because the brain is malleable in early life, these messages get hardwired.

This is supported by research on neuroplasticity and early relational trauma (Siegel, 2010; Perry & Szalavitz, 2017).

Reader:

No wonder we carry these patterns for decades.

Dr. Dubin:

And we recreate them. If I never felt validated as a child, I may unconsciously seek partners or bosses who confirm that old message. Or I may become the invalidating voice in my own head.

That's the heartbreak — and the opportunity.

Reader:

Opportunity?

Dr. Sidor:

Yes. Because once we become aware of the pattern, we can rewrite it. We can build new associations. We can learn to validate ourselves and others. But first, we have to go back to where it started – not to blame, but to reclaim our power.

Reflections and Prompts

- What messages about your emotions did you receive growing up?
- Who were the people whose responses shaped your sense of worth?
- What were you praised for? What were you criticized for?
- Can you trace your current validation-seeking patterns to early conditioning?

Practical Exercise

Your Early Validation Map

Draw a simple map of your early caregivers (parents, siblings, teachers). Next to each, write:

- What did I feel I had to be or do to earn their approval?
- What emotions or traits were encouraged? Which were dismissed?

This exercise is not about blame. It's about awareness. You are uncovering your blueprint.

Chapter 2: How It All Begins – Childhood, Conditioning, and Reinforcement

Chart: Early Validation Sources and Their Long-Term Impact

Early Validation Sources and Their Long-Term Impact

Validation Source	Example	Long-Term Impact
Parents	A child's achievements, such as a drawing or good grades, are acknowledged	Internalized self-worth through parental feedback
Caretakers	A child is praised for cooperating, following rules, or helping with chores	Sense of belonging through affirmation of behavior
Teachers	A student is commended for class participation or effort on an assignment	Motivation and confidence through academic recognition
Peers	A child receives a compliment or gains acceptance into a group	Social skills and connection through peer approval

From Mirror to Mind – How Early Reflection Becomes Internal Narrative

1. Infant observes caregiver's face and tone.
2. Repeated responses become a mirror of self-worth.
3. Child internalizes messages like "I am lovable" or "I am too much."
4. These internal messages become lifelong beliefs unless re-evaluated.

Table: Validating vs. Invalidating Phrases in Childhood

Validating Phrases	Invalidating Phrases
"It's okay to feel sad."	"Stop crying, it's not a big deal."
"I see you're upset—want to talk?"	"Don't be a baby."
"That was hard, and you did your best."	"You should've done better."
"I hear you and I understand."	"Because I said so."

Diagram: The Cycle of Conditioning

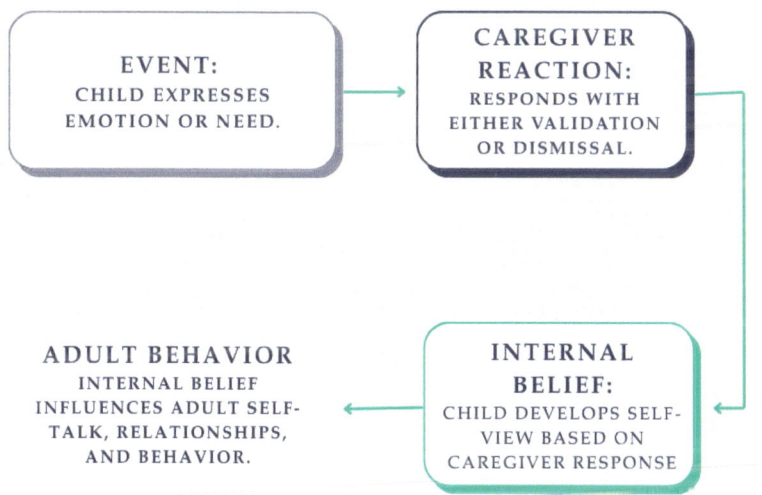

Scientific References

- Ainsworth, M. D. S. (1979). Infant–mother attachment. American Psychologist, 34(10), 932–937.
- Bowlby, J. (1988). A Secure Base: Parent-Child Attachment and Healthy Human Development. Basic Books.
- Siegel, D. J. (2010). The Developing Mind: How Relationships and the Brain Interact to Shape Who We Are. Guilford Press.
- Perry, B. D., & Szalavitz, M. (2017). The Boy Who Was Raised as a Dog: And Other Stories from a Child Psychiatrist's Notebook. Basic Books.

Chapter 3: The External Chase – Friends, Partners, Society, and the World

Scene: A busy city café. The conversation picks up as Reader, Dr. Sidor, and Dr. Dubin observe people moving through the motions of daily life—phone in hand, eyes scanning, laughter shared, glances exchanged.

Reader:

Look around—everyone here seems connected, but also like they're searching for something. Are we all chasing the same thing?

Dr. Dubin:

We are. That thing is validation. And once we leave the family system of childhood, we begin to look for it in friends, peers, romantic partners, mentors, bosses, audiences—even strangers.

Dr. Sidor:

We're wired for it. Social acceptance is tied to survival. Neuroscientific research shows that social rejection activates the same areas of the brain as physical pain (Eisenberger, Lieberman, & Williams, 2003). So we seek cues: Do they like me? Approve of me? Think I'm worthy?

Reader:

So that's why social media is so addictive?

Dr. Dubin:

Exactly. Each "like" is a dopamine hit. Each comment can feel like proof that we matter—or don't. It's not inherently bad. The problem begins when our sense of self-worth becomes entirely dependent on these external cues.

Dr. Sidor:

We adapt. Adolescents, especially, shift from parental validation to peer validation. Approval from friends becomes central to identity. The risk? If peers reject or invalidate us, it cuts deeper than ever. We may conform, suppress, or act out – all in the name of being "seen."

Studies show that peer acceptance in adolescence is a predictor of mental health in adulthood (Allen et al., 2005).

Reader:

And in adulthood?

Dr. Dubin:

The chase often continues through relationships, work, achievement, and status. A person might overwork to prove their worth to a boss; Or stay in a toxic relationship just to feel seen; Or post obsessively online seeking approval. It's all driven by a question no one dares to ask aloud: Am I enough?

Dr. Sidor:

Here's the twist – even our highest achievements can be fueled by unhealed validation wounds. That bestseller, that promotion, that political campaign – it may look like success, but deep down, it may be about earning what was never freely given.

Reader:

And if the world claps for us, but we still feel hollow inside?

Dr. Dubin:

Then we've built an identity on shaky ground. And we're terrified of losing it.

Dr. Sidor:

That's the heartbreak of external-only validation: it's unstable, unpredictable, and always requires performance. But here's the good news — once we recognize the chase, we can step off the treadmill and start building from within.

Reflections and Prompts

- What achievements or relationships in your life were driven by a need to prove your worth?
- How do you currently seek external validation (work, appearance, social media, relationships)?
- What happens when you don't receive the validation you hoped for?
- Whose opinion carries more weight than it should?

Practical Exercise

Validation Audit

For one day, track every instance where you:

- Look for a reaction
- Feel uplifted or deflated based on someone's response
- Post something online and check back for engagement

At the end of the day, reflect: What were you hoping to feel? What needs can you meet internally instead?

Chapter 3: The External Chase – Friends, Partners, Society, and the World

Infographic: The Validation Ladder

1. Childhood – Validation from parents/caregivers.
2. Adolescence – Peer approval becomes central.
3. Young Adulthood – Romantic and academic validation.
4. Adulthood – Validation from career, community, social status.
5. Society – Cultural and social norms shape identity.

Chart: Healthy External Validation vs. Unhealthy Dependency

Healthy External Validation vs. Unhealthy Dependency

Healthy External Validation	Unhealthy Dependency
Acknowledgment from others	Approval-seeking at all costs
Self-enhancement	Fear of rejection
Internal sense of worth	Relies on constant praise
Interdependent, balanced	Clingy, people-pleasing
Open and receptive	Defensive or devastated

Diagram: The Chase Cycle

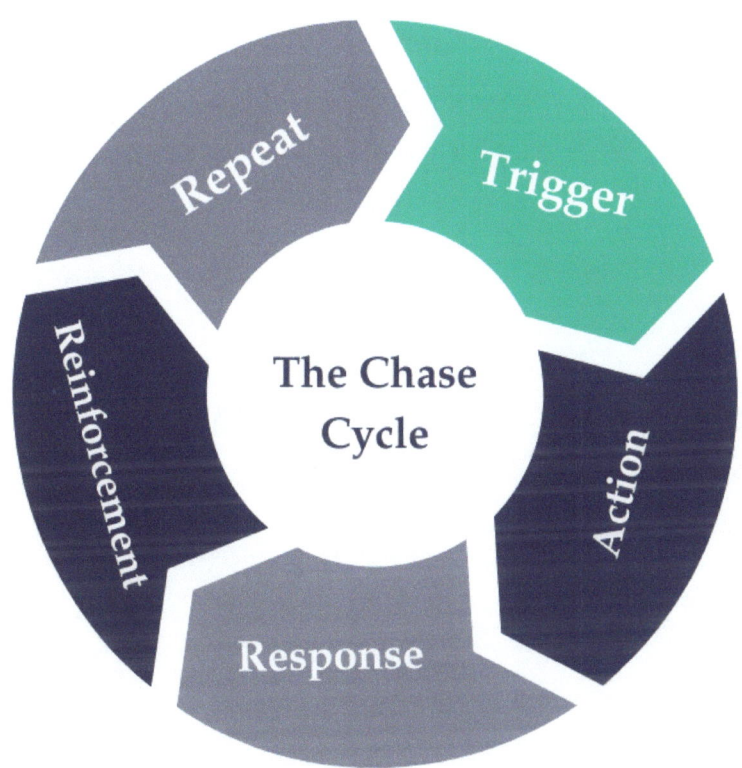

Brain Activity – Social Rejection vs. Physical Pain

Scientific research shows overlap in brain regions activated by social rejection and physical pain:

- Dorsal anterior cingulate cortex (dACC)
- Anterior insula

This supports the concept that being ignored or rejected can be neurologically painful, reinforcing our drive to seek validation.

Scientific References

- Eisenberger, N. I., Lieberman, M. D., & Williams, K. D. (2003). Does rejection hurt? An fMRI study of social exclusion. Science, 302(5643), 290-292.
- Allen, J. P., Porter, M. R., McFarland, C., Marsh, P., & McElhaney, K. B. (2005). The two faces of adolescents' success with peers: Adolescent popularity, social adaptation, and deviant behavior. Child Development, 76(3), 747–760.
- Twenge, J. M., & Campbell, W. K. (2009). The Narcissism Epidemic: Living in the Age of Entitlement. Free Press.

Chapter 4: Validation's Power – From Art to Atrocity

Scene: A quiet gallery filled with paintings and photographs. Reader stands beside Dr. Sidor and Dr. Dubin, observing a striking image—a child holding up a drawing, looking up, searching someone's face for approval.

Reader:

It's incredible, isn't it? The beauty, the longing. It makes me wonder – how much of the world's greatest art came from someone just wanting to be seen?

Dr. Dubin:

More than we can ever measure. Behind the masterpieces, the inventions, the revolutions – there's often a child who once felt invisible.

Dr. Sidor:

Validation has driven people to write symphonies, paint ceilings, launch movements, and speak truths no one else dared to say. But here's the other side: that same unmet hunger has driven others to destroy, to harm, to manipulate, to make the world feel their pain.

Reader:

So, validation isn't inherently good or bad. It just…is?

Dr. Sidor:

Exactly. Validation is like fire – it can warm a home or burn it to the ground. What matters is where it's coming from and how it's used.

Dr. Dubin:

Take Vincent van Gogh. He created some of the most significant art in history — yet he was virtually unknown in his lifetime. The need to express himself — and be validated, if only posthumously — was part of his soul's fire. On the other hand, consider those who harm others for attention, recognition, or revenge. Many acts of terror, violence, or self-destruction are rooted in a desperate need to be seen, to be heard, to say: I exist.

Reader:

Are you saying even suicide is sometimes a cry for validation?

Dr. Sidor:

Not always — but yes, often. "If I die, maybe they'll finally see me, maybe they'll finally care."

Validation is so fundamental that when it's consistently denied, the psyche can fracture.

Research by Joiner et al. (2005) shows that perceived burdensomeness and thwarted belongingness — both deeply tied to validation — are major predictors of suicidal ideation.

Dr. Dubin:

And the same is true for destructive behavior outward. If someone has been ignored, dismissed, invalidated for too long, they may explode — not because they're "evil," but because their pain had nowhere else to go. Injustice ignored is a wound that festers.

Reader:

So, what's the answer? How do we prevent this?

Dr. Sidor:

By recognizing that validation is a form of prevention. When you validate someone's experience, you interrupt a trajectory of despair. You remind them they exist, they matter, they belong.

Dr. Dubin:

And that includes ourselves. Many people either overachieve to earn validation or self-sabotage to punish themselves for not receiving it. Both are rooted in the same need.

When we learn to self-validate, we can create from love – not lack.

Reflections and Prompts

- What's something great you've done, created, or pursued out of a desire to be seen or validated?
- Have you ever acted destructively – toward yourself or others – because you felt dismissed or invisible?
- Whose recognition have you been chasing, even unconsciously?
- What would your creativity look like if it came from wholeness instead of woundedness?

Practical Exercise

Fuel Check

Think of three recent actions or decisions in your life — professional or personal. Ask yourself:

- What was the real motivation behind this?
- Was I seeking to be seen, to belong, to prove something?
- If I already felt worthy, would I still have made the same choice?

Use this awareness to begin realigning your energy from validation-seeking to authentic expression.

Chapter 4: Validation's Power – From Art to Atrocity

Infographic: The Double-Edged Power of Validation

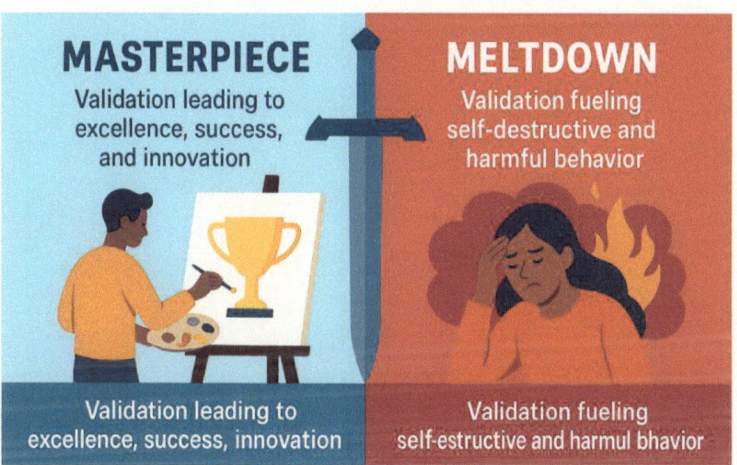

This infographic shows two branches stemming from the core human need for validation—highlighting how unmet needs may lead to creativity or catastrophe depending on internal and external support.

Chart: Creative vs. Destructive Validation Responses

Creative Responses to Validation Needs	Destructive Responses to Validation Needs
Writing or creating art	Violence or aggression
Helping others or mentoring	Manipulation or control
Speaking out for justice	Lashing out or isolating
Channeling pain into activism	Self-harm or revenge

Diagram: The Pain-to-Action Pathway

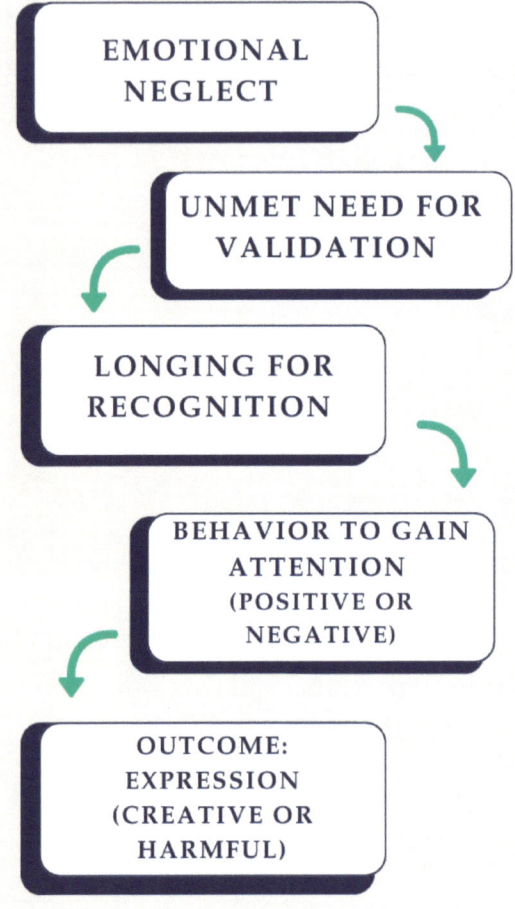

This diagram explains how unmet emotional needs can evolve into outward actions—some healing, some harmful—depending on support and environment.

Suicide and Aggression – Two Sides of Unmet Validation

Unmet validation can manifest inward (suicide) or outward (aggression):

INWARD → feelings of invisibility, shame, worthlessness → withdrawal, depression, suicidality

OUTWARD → rage, desperation, need to be noticed → aggression, violence, harm to others

Supportive validation disrupts this trajectory and promotes healing.

Scientific References

- Joiner, T. E. (2005). Why People Die by Suicide. Harvard University Press.
- Baumeister, R. F. (1990). Suicide as escape from self. Psychological Review, 97(1), 90–113.
- Twenge, J. M., Baumeister, R. F., DeWall, C. N., Ciarocco, N. J., & Bartels, J. M. (2007). Social exclusion causes self-defeating behavior. Journal of Personality and Social Psychology, 92(1), 56–66.
- Neimeyer, R. A. (2000). Searching for the meaning of meaning: Grief therapy and the process of reconstruction. Death Studies, 24(6), 541–558.

Chapter 5: When It Stops Working – The Crisis of Misplaced Worth

Scene: A quiet office late at night. The Reader sits across from Dr. Dubin and Dr. Sidor, a cup of tea in hand, the energy shifted from curiosity to quiet honesty.

Reader:

I've followed every rule, I worked hard, I made people proud, and I tried to be everything to everyone. And still… something's off.

Why does it feel like I'm constantly chasing something that never lasts?

Dr. Dubin:

Because it never does. External validation is powerful – but it's also fleeting. It's like trying to fill a well with water that evaporates faster than you can pour.

Dr. Sidor:

We call this the crisis of misplaced worth – when you've built your identity around being validated by others, and then suddenly, the applause stops, or it doesn't land the same way. Or worse, you succeed and still feel empty.

Reader:

It's like I built my self-worth on sand.

Dr. Dubin:

You're not alone. So many people follow the script: achieve, please, perfect, perform – and then collapse under the weight of a question they never dared ask:

What if none of this makes me truly feel whole?

Dr. Sidor:

The danger of misplaced validation is not just emotional — it's neurological and behavioral. It wires us for conditional self-regard. We only feel good when someone else says we are.

Research by Deci & Ryan (2000) shows that externally controlled motivation leads to decreased well-being, reduced intrinsic motivation, and even increased anxiety and depression over time.

When our self-worth is tethered to approval, we become slaves to perception.

Dr. Dubin:

And it shows up in subtle and not-so-subtle ways. The person who's afraid to say no. The partner who bends to please but feels resentful. The high-achiever who's exhausted but can't stop. The social media influencer who spirals after one negative comment.

These aren't character flaws — they're symptoms of misaligned validation.

Reader:

So, what happens when people hit this wall — when validation stops working?

Dr. Sidor:

One of three things usually happens:

1. **Collapse**: *They give up, spiral into self-doubt, depression, or shame.*
2. **Escalation**: *They work harder, louder, more intensely to earn what they've lost.*

3. ***Awakening***: *They begin to question the foundation and search inward instead.*

Reader:

That third one… is that the way out?

Dr. Dubin:

It's the beginning. But first comes grief — grieving the time, energy, and identity we built chasing what we thought would make us feel complete. That grief is painful — but it's also precious. It clears the ground for something new.

Dr. Sidor:

Here's the good news: Worth is never truly lost. It's only misplaced. And you can reclaim it — not through others, but through a quiet, steady practice of self-validation.

Reflections and Prompts

- Have you ever achieved something and still felt "not enough"?
- In what areas of life are you performing more than being?
- Who or what have you given too much power to define your worth?
- What would change if your validation came from within?

Practical Exercise

The Worth Reclamation Letter

Write a letter to yourself from your future, self-validated self. Let them remind you that your worth was never dependent on a title, a relationship, a follower count, or a performance. Let this letter speak from truth — not fear.

Keep it somewhere visible. Read it every morning for one week.

Chapter 5: When It Stops Working – The Crisis of Misplaced Worth

Infographic: The Cycle of Misplaced Worth

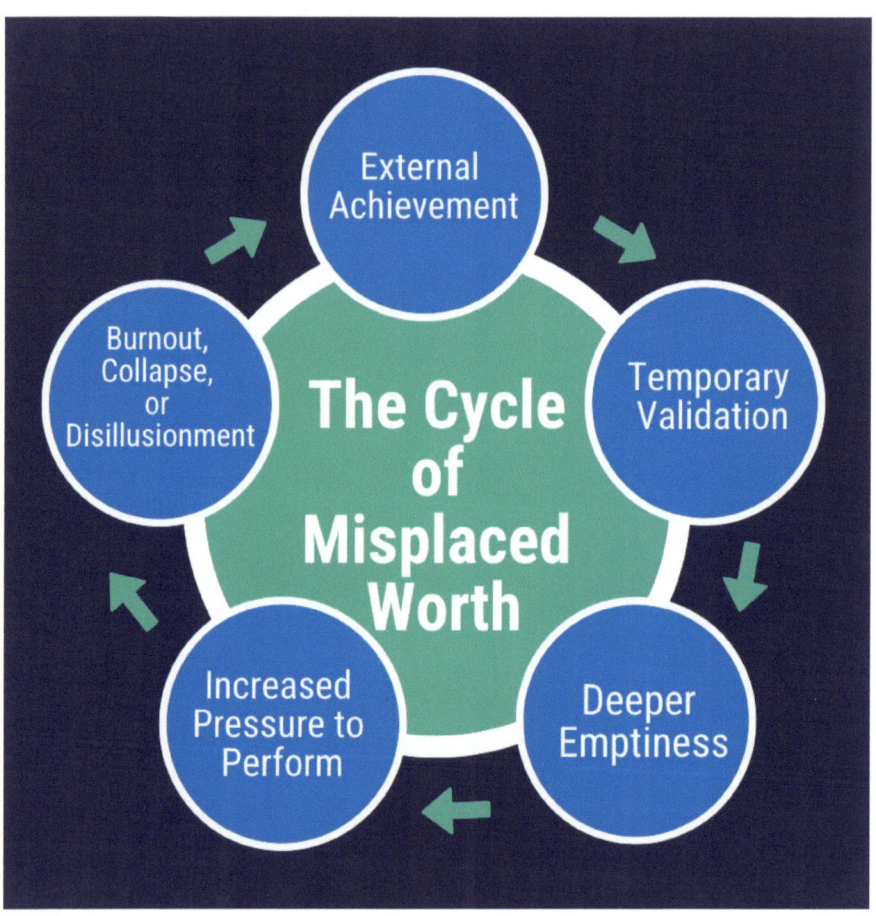

This cycle illustrates how relying solely on external validation can lead to a hollow sense of worth.

Chart: External vs. Internal Validation

External Validation vs. Internal Validation

External Validation (Short-Term Relief)	Internal Validation (Long-Term Peace)
• Based on others' approval	Based on self-acceptance
• Temporary and fleeting	Enduring and stable
• Driven by achievement	Rooted in self-worth

Diagram: Responses to Validation Collapse

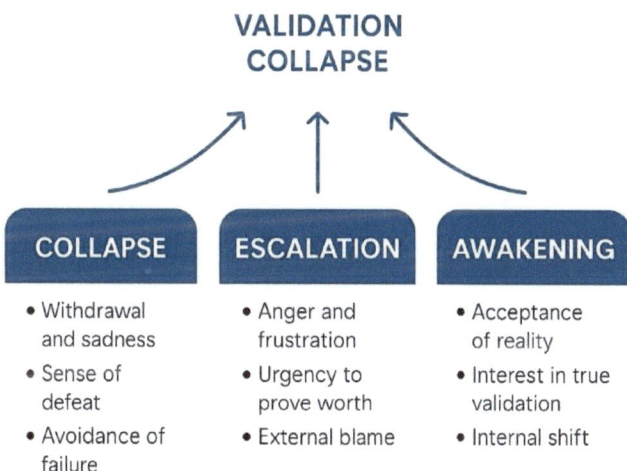

These paths demonstrate how people respond when their external validation strategies break down.

Signs of Misplaced Worth

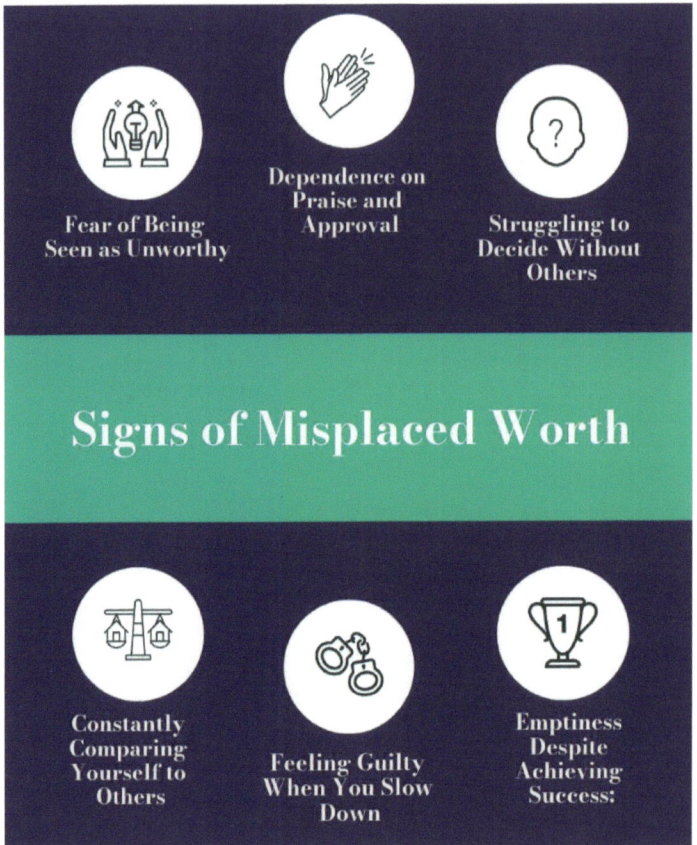

Scientific References

- Deci, E. L., & Ryan, R. M. (2000). The "what" and "why" of goal pursuits: Human needs and the self-determination of behavior. Psychological Inquiry, 11(4), 227–268.
- Crocker, J., & Wolfe, C. T. (2001). Contingencies of self-worth. Psychological Review, 108(3), 593–623.
- Neff, K. D. (2011). Self-Compassion: The Proven Power of Being Kind to Yourself. William Morrow.

Chapter 6: Turning Inward – Discovering the Source Within

Scene: A candlelit meditation studio. The room is quiet. Reader sits cross-legged on a cushion across from Dr. Sidor and Dr. Dubin. The external noise has softened. The conversation turns inward.

Reader:

Okay... I see it now. I've been outsourcing my worth for most of my life. But how do I stop? How do I start validating myself?

Dr. Sidor:

That question – right there – is the beginning of your transformation.

Dr. Dubin:

Self-validation isn't an event, it's a practice. It means learning to become your own mirror, your own source of "I see you, I hear you, and you make sense."

Reader:

That sounds... hard. What if I don't believe it yet?

Dr. Sidor:

That's normal. Most of us were never taught this. We were conditioned to seek approval, not self-recognition. But neuroscience tells us we can rewire that pattern.

Studies show that practices like mindfulness, self-compassion, and self-affirming statements stimulate the prefrontal cortex and reduce activity in the brain's threat system (Neff, 2011; Siegel, 2010).

Dr. Dubin:

Let's start simple. Imagine your inner voice as a child who just wants to be acknowledged. What would you say if you were trying to comfort that child?

Reader (quietly):

"I know you're trying… and I'm proud of you."

Dr. Sidor:

Beautiful. That's self-validation.

Dr. Dubin:

And it expands from there:

- *"My feelings make sense."*
- *"I'm allowed to take up space."*
- *"I can choose to belong to myself before belonging to anyone else."*

Reader:

But won't people think I'm selfish or arrogant?

Dr. Dubin:

Self-validation isn't arrogance. Arrogance is rooted in insecurity. True self-validation is humble. It doesn't need to prove anything – it just knows.

Dr. Sidor:

And ironically, the more you validate yourself, the more you can show up for others without needing something from them. You stop performing, and you start being. That's when relationships shift, work becomes sustainable, and peace becomes real.

Reflections and Prompts

- What are the most common things you say to yourself when you make a mistake?
- What would it sound like to validate your feelings instead of judging them?
- Can you recall a moment when you could have validated yourself — but didn't?
- What's one phrase of self-validation you want to start saying daily?

Practical Exercise

Self-Validation Mirror Practice

Each morning, look at yourself in the mirror and say:

- "I see you."
- "I hear you."
- "Your experience matters."
- "You are enough."

Repeat for 7 days. Even if it feels awkward, do it anyway. You're not lying to yourself; rather, you're remembering the truth.

Chapter 6: Turning Inward – Discovering the Source Within

THE ANATOMY OF SELF-VALIDATION

THOUGHTS

- I am enough
- It's okay to make mistakes
- I am learning and growing

EMOTIONS

- I feel what I feel
- My emotions matter
- I accept myself as I am

BEHAVIORS

- I set healthy boundaries
- I speak to myself with kindness
- I honor my needs

These interconnected systems demonstrate how self-validation influences whole-person wellbeing.

Table: Self-Validation Phrases vs. Internal Criticism

Self-Validation Phrases	Internal Criticism
I did my best	I should have done better
It's okay to make mistakes	I can't believe I messed up
I am enough as I am	I'm not good enough
I trust myself to figure this out	I always mess things up
My feelings are valid	I shouldn't feel this way
I handled that well given the circumstances	I should have known better
I am proud of what I've accomplished	What I've done isn't that important
I deserve kindness and respect	I don't deserve to be treated well
I am growing and learning	I'll never get this right

Diagram: Brain Pathways Activated by Self-Compassion

Practices like mindful self-talk and mirror work activate:

- Prefrontal Cortex: Emotional regulation, decision making
- Anterior Cingulate Cortex: Empathy and social connection
- Ventral Striatum: Reward and self-recognition

These regions support psychological resilience and reduce shame.

Chart: Internal vs. External Validation Effects

INTERNAL vs. EXTERNAL VALIDATION

INTERNAL VALIDATION	EXTERNAL VALIDATION
Stable and inherent	Fluctuating and contingent
Adaptive and enduring	Fragile and dependent
Authentic and boundaried	Transactional and conditional
Effects on Self-Worth, Resilience	

Scientific References

- Neff, K. D. (2011). Self-Compassion: The Proven Power of Being Kind to Yourself. William Morrow.
- Siegel, D. J. (2010). The Mindful Therapist: A Clinician's Guide to Mindsight and Neural Integration. W. W. Norton.
- Gilbert, P., & Procter, S. (2006). Compassionate mind training for people with high shame and self-criticism. Clinical Psychology & Psychotherapy, 13(6), 353–379.
- Shapiro, S. L., Brown, K. W., & Biegel, G. M. (2007). Teaching self-care to caregivers: Effects of mindfulness-based stress reduction on the mental health of therapists in training. Training and Education in Professional Psychology, 1(2), 105–115.

Chapter 7: The Practice of Self-Validation – Tools for Everyday Life

Scene: A sun-drenched kitchen table. Dr. Dubin and Dr. Sidor sit with Reader, a notebook open, pens in hand, as they create a toolkit together.

Reader:

Okay, I get it. Self-validation is essential. I'm starting to believe it's possible.

But how do I actually live it – when the world is loud, fast, and full of judgment?

Dr. Sidor:

Like anything worth mastering, it's a daily practice. Self-validation isn't a feeling you wait for – it's a behavior you choose; and over time, that behavior changes your beliefs.

Dr. Dubin:

*Let's start with the **Three Pillars of Self-Validation**:*

1. *Acknowledge Your Internal Experience*
2. *Normalize It Without Judgment*
3. *Respond with Compassion*

Reader:

Sounds like a kind of internal conversation.

Dr. Dubin:

Exactly. For example:

- *"I feel overwhelmed." (acknowledge)*
- *"It makes sense – today has been hard." (normalize)*
- *"Let me give myself a moment to breathe." (respond with compassion)*

Dr. Sidor:

And when practiced regularly, it builds emotional regulation, resilience, and self-trust.

Research confirms that self-validation improves psychological flexibility and reduces rumination (Kross et al., 2011; Neff & Germer, 2013).

Reader:

What are some other ways to practice?

Six Core Practices of Self-Validation

1. **Name the Feeling**
   "I feel anxious." "I'm sad." "I'm frustrated."
   Naming the emotion activates the prefrontal cortex and reduces emotional intensity.
2. **Say "It Makes Sense"**
   Even if you wish you felt differently, say: "It makes sense I feel this way because…"
   (This interrupts the inner critic and builds internal safety.)
3. **Pause Before Fixing or Judging**
   Don't rush to solve or silence your emotions. Sit with them as a compassionate witness.

4. **Breathe and Anchor**
   Bring awareness to your breath. Validate your right to slow down and feel.
5. **Affirm Your Humanity**
   "This is hard—and I'm doing my best." "I am allowed to feel, struggle, and still be worthy."
6. **Write a Validation Note to Yourself**

   Just a few lines:

   "Dear [Your Name], I see you. I know this is tough. And I'm proud of you for showing up."

Reader:

What if I mess up? Or I forget?

Dr. Sidor:

That's part of it. Every time you return to the practice, even after forgetting, you are validating yourself again. That's the point.

Dr. Dubin:

Self-validation isn't perfection; rather, it's presence.

Reflections and Prompts

- What's your default inner response when something goes wrong?
- What parts of yourself are you most reluctant to validate?
- Which of the six practices feels easiest to try first? Which one feels hardest?

Practical Exercise

30-Second Validation Reset

When you feel dysregulated, pause and say out loud (or silently):

- "This is how I feel."
- "It makes sense."
- "I'm allowed to feel this."

Repeat 3 times. This micro-practice builds the muscle of compassion under pressure.

Chapter 7: The Practice of Self-Validation – Tools for Everyday Life

Infographic: The Three Pillars of Self-Validation

Chart: Six Core Practices and Their Effects

Core Practice	Why It Works
Name the feeling	Increases emotional clarity and regulation
Say 'It makes sense'	Reduces self-blame and internal shame
Pause before fixing	Creates space for awareness and self-acceptance
Breathe and anchor	Activates calm, grounded state
Affirm your humanity	Builds self-compassion and worth
Write a validation note	Transforms inner narrative and reinforces truth

Table: Internal Critic vs. Self-Validation

Common Internal Critic Phrases vs. Self-Validation Responses	
Common Internal Critic Phrases	Self-Valldation Responses
I'm not good enough.	I'm doing my best, and that's enough.
I always mess things up.	Everyone makes mistakes; I'm learning and growing.
Nobody cares what I have to say.	I have a voice that matters.
I should be better by now.	I'm proud of the progress I've made.
I don't deserve this.	I am worthy of good things.
I don't deserve this.	I am worthy of good things.

Checklist: Daily Self-Validation Practice Tracker

- [ ] I named my feelings today.
- [ ] I said "It makes sense I feel this way."
- [ ] I responded to myself with kindness.
- [ ] I paused before judging myself.
- [ ] I reminded myself of my humanity.
- [ ] I offered myself encouragement or rest.

Scientific References

- Kross, E., et al. (2011). Self-talk as a regulatory mechanism: How you do it matters. Journal of Personality and Social Psychology, 101(2), 263–280.
- Neff, K. D., & Germer, C. K. (2013). A pilot study and randomized controlled trial of the Mindful Self-Compassion program. Journal of Clinical Psychology, 69(1), 28–44.
- Linehan, M. M. (1993). Skills Training Manual for Treating Borderline Personality Disorder. Guilford Press.
- Arch, J. J., & Craske, M. G. (2006). Mechanisms of mindfulness: Emotion regulation following a focused breathing induction. Behaviour Research and Therapy, 44(12), 1849–1858.

Chapter 8: Learning to Listen – Inner Voice, Inner Child, Inner Truth

Scene: A warm, softly lit room. Reader sits with Dr. Sidor and Dr. Dubin around a small table, where crayons and old childhood photos rest beside cups of tea. The conversation turns from behavior to identity—from outer practices to inner presence.

Reader:

Sometimes, when I try to validate myself, another voice shows up—sarcastic, dismissive, even cruel.

It tells me I'm being dramatic or weak.

How do I deal with that voice?

Dr. Dubin:

That voice is part of your inner system—it formed to protect you. It may have taken on the tone of a parent, teacher, peer, or culture that didn't know how to validate. But you're not stuck with it. You can learn to hear beneath it.

Dr. Sidor:

We all have multiple inner voices.

There's the inner critic—harsh and familiar.

The inner child—vulnerable and longing.

And the inner truth—calm, steady, and wise.

Validation begins when we learn to recognize them, listen with curiosity, and choose which one leads.

Reader:

So, the inner critic isn't the enemy?

Dr. Dubin:

No. It's a scared part of you trying to keep you safe by preventing vulnerability. But healing begins when we say, "Thank you for trying to protect me. But I've got this now."

Dr. Sidor:

And then you turn toward the voice that hasn't been heard enough – the inner child who once asked, "Do I matter?" That child still exists within you, waiting to be met with love.

The Inner Validation Process (adapted from IFS and Schema Therapy)

1. **Pause** – When emotion rises, stop and listen.
2. **Ask** – "Who in me is speaking right now?"
3. **Name** – "This sounds like my inner critic… or my 7-year-old self… or my anxious part."
4. **Validate** – "It makes sense that you feel this way."
5. **Respond from the Wise Self** – Calmly, kindly, and with clarity.

Reader:

How do I know I'm hearing my "inner truth" and not just fear disguised as wisdom?

Dr. Sidor:

The inner truth voice feels like grounded knowing. It's firm, not frantic. It is kind, not indulgent. It doesn't argue – it guides.

It often speaks quietly, which is why we need stillness to hear it.

Dr. Dubin:

Journaling, breathwork, meditation, and inner dialogue exercises help create that stillness.

When you practice enough, your inner truth becomes a companion — not a stranger.

Reflections and Prompts

- What does your inner critic often say? Whose voice does it resemble?
- What might your inner child still need to hear today?
- Can you recall a moment when your inner truth guided you?
- What practices help you slow down enough to truly listen inwardly?

Practical Exercise

The Inner Child Letter

Write a short letter to your younger self — any age that feels relevant.

Begin with: "Dear [Your Name], I see you. I know how hard that was. I want you to know…"

Read it aloud to yourself; and keep it. You can come back to it any time you forget your worth.

Chapter 8: Learning to Listen – Inner Voice, Inner Child, Inner Truth

The Three Inner Voices

- **Inner Critic**: Harsh, protective, often echoes external judgment.
- **Inner Child**: Vulnerable, emotional, seeks safety and love.
- **Inner Truth**: Grounded, wise, calm, and non-reactive.

Understanding each voice helps you respond from your center rather than react from your conditioning.

Table:

What Each Voice Says vs. What It Needs

Inner Voice	What It Says	What It Needs
Critic	You're not good enough.	Acceptance and compassion
Child	I'm scared and alone.	Safety and reassurance
Truth	I'm whole and worthy.	Acknowledgment and presence

Shifting from Inner Critic to Inner Truth

1. Hear the Critic – Recognize the voice.
2. Identify the Fear – Ask what the critic is protecting.
3. Offer Validation – "I hear you, and I choose to be kind."
4. Listen for Inner Truth – Breathe, slow down, reflect.
5. Speak from Wisdom – Respond with compassion and clarity.

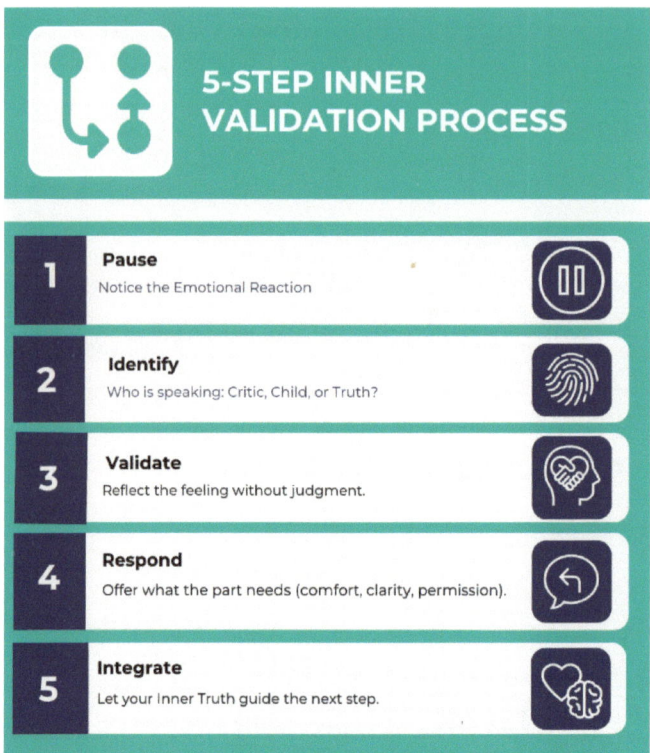

Scientific References

- Schwartz, R. C. (2001). Internal Family Systems Therapy. Guilford Press.
- Young, J. E., Klosko, J. S., & Weishaar, M. E. (2003). Schema Therapy: A Practitioner's Guide. Guilford Press.
- Neff, K. D. (2003). The development and validation of a scale to measure self-compassion. Self and Identity, 2(3), 223–250.
- Geller, S. M., & Greenberg, L. S. (2002). Therapeutic presence: Therapists' experience of presence in the psychotherapy encounter. Person-Centered & Experiential Psychotherapies, 1(1–2), 71–86.

Chapter 9: Mirror Work, Journaling, and the Neuroscience of Worth

Scene: A quiet morning. Reader sits with Dr. Dubin and Dr. Sidor in a softly lit space with a journal, a mirror, and a sense that something precious is about to begin.

Reader:

I've been thinking a lot about what we talked about last time – about that inner child.

However, I still struggle to believe the things I say to myself. It feels… forced.

Dr. Dubin:

That's normal. Most people were never taught to look at themselves and say, "You are enough." That's why we need practices that make it real – in the body, the nervous system, the mind. Two of the most powerful are mirror work and reflective journaling.

Dr. Sidor:

And there's a neuroscience to it. When you look into your own eyes and offer compassion, or when you write to yourself from a place of truth, you create new neural pathways.

Studies show that self-affirming practices increase activity in the brain's reward centers and reduce stress-related activation in the amygdala (Cascio et al., 2016).

Part 1: Mirror Work – Making Eye Contact with the Self

What It Is:

Mirror work is the act of looking into your own eyes and speaking words of truth, compassion, and validation. It may feel awkward at first, but over time, it becomes a pathway to self-intimacy and integration.

How to Practice:

1. Stand or sit in front of a mirror.
2. Breathe deeply. Ground yourself.
3. Look directly into your own eyes.
4. Say one or more of the following phrases:
    a. "I see you."
    b. "You are doing your best."
    c. "You're allowed to feel this."
    d. "You matter. You always have."
5. Pause. Notice the sensations in your body.

Dr. Dubin:

The mirror bypasses the rational mind and connects with something deeper. You're not just thinking – you're seeing and being seen.

Part 2: Journaling – Writing the Inner Voice into Clarity

What It Is:

Journaling externalizes thoughts and emotions so you can examine, validate, and reframe them. It's like holding a mirror to the mind.

Core Self-Validation Journal Prompts:

- "Today, I felt ___, and it makes sense because ___."
- "A part of me believes ___. I want to tell that part…"
- "I handled ___ today, and I'm proud of myself for…"
- "Dear younger me, I want you to know…"
- "Dear future me, I promise…"

Dr. Sidor:

Writing is a neurological act. It integrates right and left brain processes and helps transform unspoken emotion into conscious experience. That's where healing begins.

Reader:

It feels strange… but also like something I've needed my whole life.

Dr. Dubin:

It's not strange — it's precious. You're meeting yourself with the same kindness you've been waiting for from the world.

Dr. Sidor:

And each time you write or speak that truth, your brain rewires; and bit by bit, the old scripts fade — and something wiser takes root.

Reflections and Prompts

- What emotions come up when you look into your own eyes in the mirror?
- What would it mean to become someone who truly sees and hears themselves?
- What limiting belief about your worth are you ready to rewrite?

Practical Exercise

7-Day Mirror + Journal Practice

Each day for one week:

1. Spend 2 minutes looking into your eyes in the mirror. Say 2 validating phrases.
2. Spend 5–10 minutes journaling a response to one of the prompts above.

Track any emotional shifts or resistance. These are signs of change.

Chapter 9: Mirror Work, Journaling, and the Neuroscience of Worth

Infographic: How Mirror Work Changes the Brain

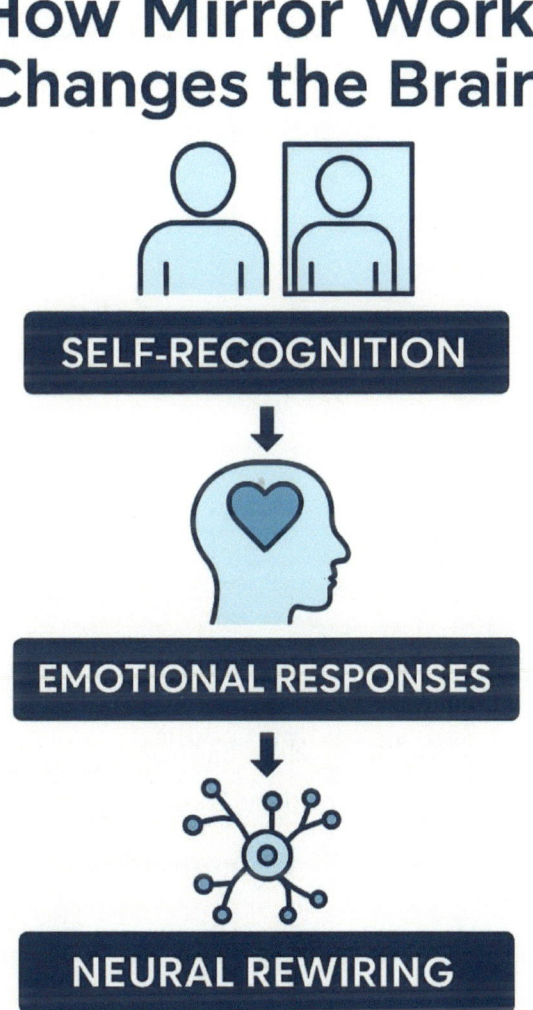

Practicing mirror work strengthens positive self-perception and emotional integration.

Chart: Mirror Work vs. Avoidance – Emotional Outcomes

MIRROR WORK VS. AVOIDANCE:
Emotional Outcomes

MIRROR WORK	AVOIDANCE
Self-acceptance	Insecurity
Increased self-worth	Criticism
Emotional clarity	Avoidance
Self-reflection	Denial
Boosted confidence	Shame
Emotional healing	Distress

The Journal-to-Self-Validation Feedback Loop

1. Express thoughts and emotions in writing ➔

2. See yourself with honesty and curiosity ➔

3. Validate the experience ("It makes sense I feel this") ➔

4. Feel seen and soothed internally ➔

5. Strengthen neural patterns of self-compassion and worth ➔

6. Repeat – rewiring identity over time.

Table: Journal Prompts and Emotional Needs

Journal Prompt	Emotional Need
"Today I felt ___, and it makes sense because…"	Emotional recognition and safety
"Dear younger me, I want you to know…"	Healing and affirmation
"One thing I'm learning about myself is…"	Self-awareness and growth
"If I truly trusted myself, I would…"	Empowerment and direction

Scientific References

- Cascio, C. N., O'Donnell, M. B., Tinney, F. J., Lieberman, M. D., Taylor, S. E., Strecher, V. J., & Falk, E. B. (2016). Self-affirmation activates the ventral striatum: A possible reward-related mechanism for self-affirmation. Psychological Science, 27(4), 455–466.
- Pennebaker, J. W., & Seagal, J. D. (1999). Forming a story: The health benefits of narrative. Journal of Clinical Psychology, 55(10), 1243–1254.
- Neff, K. D., & Germer, C. K. (2013). The Mindful Self-Compassion Workbook. Guilford Press.
- Siegel, D. J. (2010). The Mindful Brain: Reflection and Attunement in the Cultivation of Well-Being. Norton.

Chapter 10: Rewiring the Brain – How Internal Validation Reshapes Us

Scene: A neuroscience lab meets a meditation space. Reader, Dr. Sidor, and Dr. Dubin gather around a brain scan image glowing on a screen. Instead of just circuits and synapses, they see story, identity, and possibility.

Reader:

So, you're telling me… validation isn't just emotional – it's neurological?

Dr. Sidor:

Absolutely. Our brains are shaped by what we repeatedly do and say to ourselves. If you've spent a lifetime judging, suppressing, or dismissing your experience, those neural pathways are well-worn highways. But every time you practice internal validation, you're paving a new road.

Dr. Dubin:

And here's the miracle of neuroplasticity: The brain doesn't care how old you are. It just needs repetition and intention.

How Validation Rewires the Brain

1. **Decreases Activity in the Threat System**
   Self-validation lowers activity in the amygdala, reducing fear, shame, and self-blame. (Goldin et al., 2009)
2. **Activates the Prefrontal Cortex**
   This part of the brain supports reflection, emotional regulation, and self-awareness. (Creswell et al., 2013)

3. **Stimulates the Reward System**
   When we validate ourselves, we activate the ventral striatum, reinforcing healthy self-perception. (Cascio et al., 2016)
4. **Strengthens Neural Integration**
   Practices like mindful self-talk and journaling enhance connectivity between brain hemispheres, linking logic with emotion, thought with feeling. (Siegel, 2010)

Reader:

So, I really can change how I feel, by changing how I speak to myself?

Dr. Dubin:

Yes — and more. You change who you believe yourself to be.

That's the real power of internal validation — it doesn't just make you feel better for a moment. It helps you become someone who no longer doubts their right to exist, to feel, to belong.

Dr. Sidor:

You build self-trust, you reclaim authority over your emotional life, you stop chasing worth, and start embodying it.

The Brain on Validation vs. Invalidation

Brain Area	Validation Effect	Invalidation Effect
Amygdala	Calms fear, decreases reactivity	Triggers fight/flight/freeze
Prefrontal Cortex	Supports regulation and insight	Deactivates under chronic stress
Ventral Striatum	Reinforced healthy self-belief	Craves external reward and attention
Insula	Enhances emotional awareness	Can become numb or hypersensitive

Reflections and Prompts

- What beliefs about your worth have been hardwired through past experiences?
- Which of those beliefs are you now ready to rewrite?
- What would it mean to trust your own emotions—not as weakness, but as wisdom?

Practical Exercise

The Rewiring Ritual – 21 Days of Internal Validation

Each morning:

1. Place your hand on your heart.
2. Say out loud:
    a. "I am safe with myself."
    b. "I can trust my feelings."
    c. "I validate my truth."
3. Write one short sentence of self-validation in your journal.

Repeat this for 21 days. Science shows this is long enough to begin reshaping brain pathways.

Chapter 10: Rewiring the Brain – How Internal Validation Reshapes Us

The Brain on Validation

- **Prefrontal Cortex**: Enhances regulation and mindfulness
- **Anterior Cingulate Cortex**: Fosters empathy and self-awareness
- **Ventral Striatum**: Activates reward and motivation pathways
- **Amygdala**: Deactivates during self-compassion, lowering stress

Internal validation reshapes the brain to support emotional safety and resilience.

Chart: Neuroplasticity Timeline

Time Frame	Neuroplastic Impact of Validation Practice
Day 1–7	Initial awareness and emotional softening
Week 2–3	Reduced self-judgment, new pathways forming
Week 4–6	Increased access to self-regulation and self-trust
Beyond 6 weeks	Reinforced identity and lasting resilience

From Criticism to Compassion – Neural Pathway Rewiring

Old Pathway:

Trigger → Inner Critic → Shame → Emotional Shutdown

New Pathway:

Trigger → Acknowledgment → Self-Validation → Regulation and Growth

Repetition of the second path strengthens emotional flexibility and resilience.

From Practice to Identity Integration

Daily Practice → Activates supportive brain regions → Reinforces self-compassion → Shapes internal narrative → Develops secure identity → Internal validation becomes default response.

Scientific References

- Goldin, P. R., et al. (2009). The neural bases of emotion regulation: Reappraisal and suppression of negative emotion. Biological Psychiatry, 65(5), 367–373.
- Cascio, C. N., et al. (2016). Self-affirmation activates the ventral striatum. Psychological Science, 27(4), 455–466.
- Siegel, D. J. (2010). The Mindful Therapist. W. W. Norton & Company.
- Creswell, J. D., et al. (2013). Neural reactivity to emotional stimuli and resilience. Emotion, 13(5), 1091–1098.
- Davidson, R. J., & McEwen, B. S. (2012). Social influences on neuroplasticity: Stress and interventions to promote well-being. Nature Neuroscience, 15(5), 689–695.

Chapter 11: Validating Others – Every Interaction as an Opportunity

Scene: A community center. Reader stands beside Dr. Dubin and Dr. Sidor, observing staff speaking to residents, peers, and children. Some voices are warm, some are sharp, and some are distracted. The trio watches with deep attention.

Reader:

I've been thinking... if validation has changed me this much, what would happen if everyone started doing this for each other?

Dr. Dubin:

The world would shift – relationship by relationship. Validation isn't just personal, it's relational medicine, it repairs disconnection, it restores dignity, and it transforms shame into safety.

Dr. Sidor:

Every interaction is a chance. Every word, glance, response is an invitation to say: You matter, I see you, you're allowed to be you right now. And the absence of that? It leaves a mark.

The Five Golden Moments for Validation

1. **When Someone Shares Pain**

    Instead of fixing: "That sounds so hard. I could get why you feel that way."

2. **When Emotions Run High**

    Before calming down: "It makes sense that you're upset."

3. **When Someone Feels Invisible**

   Bring them in: "I want to hear what you think."

4. **When There's Conflict**

   Acknowledge first: "I can understand why that frustrated you."

5. **When You Disagree**

   Even then: "I can see how, from your perspective, that makes sense."

Reader:

So, this works even when I don't agree?

Dr. Sidor:

Especially then. Validation doesn't mean approval. It means acknowledgment. You're saying, Your experience is valid, even if I don't share it.

Dr. Dubin:

It's the foundation of psychological safety. Whether you're a therapist, parent, teacher, or supervisor — validation opens the door for trust; and trust changes everything.

What Happens When We Validate Others

- They feel seen, not judged
- Their nervous system relaxes
- Shame transforms into self-awareness
- Connection becomes possible
- Defensiveness dissolves
- They begin to validate themselves

Neuroscience shows that being validated reduces cortisol and activates the vagus nerve, promoting calm and connectedness (Porges, 2011).

Reflections and Prompts

- Who in your life has made you feel truly seen? What did they do or say?
- When have you unintentionally invalidated someone?
- What relationship would change if validation became your first response?

Practical Exercise

The 3-Second Validation Pause

Next time someone shares something — good, bad, neutral — pause for 3 seconds before you respond.

In that pause, silently ask yourself: What part of this deserves to be seen or acknowledged?

Then reflect it back, even briefly:

- "That took courage to say."
- "I can tell this really matters to you."
- "You've been holding a lot."

Chapter 11: Validating Others – Every Interaction as an Opportunity

Infographic: The Five Golden Moments for Validation

1. When someone shares pain – "That sounds really hard."
2. When emotions run high – "I can get why this is so upsetting."
3. When someone feels invisible – "I value what you have to say."
4. When there's conflict – "I can understand your frustration."
5. When you disagree – "Your perspective still matters."

Chart: Validation vs. Invalidation in Speech

Validation vs. Invalidation in Everyday Speech

Validation	Invalidation
I can see why you feel that way.	You shouldn't feel like that.
That must have been difficult for you	It's not that big of a deal.
What would be helpful for you right now?	You'd be fine if you just did it my way.
I want to understand your point of view	You're overreacting again.
Tell me more about what happened	This is just like you to mess up

Diagram: The Ripple Effect of Validation

Validation → Person feels seen → Emotional safety increases → Trust deepens → Openness expands → Cycle continues with others.

A single validating act creates waves of connection and belonging across relationships and environments.

Checklist: Daily Validation Prompts

DAILY VALIDATION PROMPTS
FOR WORK, FAMILY, AND COMMUNITY

CHECKLIST

- [ ] Have I acknowledged someone's feelings or efforts?
- [ ] Have I shown appreciation for another's perspective?
- [ ] Have I recognized a small win or shared a moment of joy?
- [ ] Have I offered encouragement or support during a challenge?
- [ ] Have I made someone feel understood or valued
- [ ] Have I...

Scientific References

- Porges, S. W. (2011). The Polyvagal Theory: Neurophysiological Foundations of Emotions, Attachment, Communication, and Self-Regulation. Norton.
- Rogers, C. R. (1961). On Becoming a Person: A Therapist's View of Psychotherapy. Houghton Mifflin.
- Siegel, D. J., & Bryson, T. P. (2011). The Whole-Brain Child. Delacorte Press.
- Linehan, M. M. (1993). Cognitive-Behavioral Treatment of Borderline Personality Disorder. Guilford Press.

Chapter 12: Modeling Validation – At Work, Home, and in Leadership

Scene: A team meeting room. Reader, Dr. Sidor, and Dr. Dubin observe a heated discussion between staff. Tension rises, voices get sharper, but something shifts when one team member pauses and says, "I hear you. I can see where you're coming from." The room changes.

Reader:

That one sentence changed the room. It was like everyone exhaled.

Dr. Dubin:

That's the power of modeled validation. When one person practices it, it gives others permission to do the same. Whether you're a parent, supervisor, therapist, or friend – how you speak becomes how others feel.

Dr. Sidor:

Leadership isn't about position – it's about presence. And one of the most influential forms of presence is the ability to validate. It creates psychological safety, team cohesion, and emotional accountability.

What Modeling Validation Looks Like

In Families:

- "I can see you're upset – and your feelings are okay."
- "Thank you for telling me how you feel."

In Teams:
- "You've clearly put a lot of thought into this. I appreciate that."
- "It's okay to not have all the answers. Let's work through this together."

In Leadership:
- "I see how hard this decision is."
- "Your perspective is important, even if the outcome won't change."

In Mentorship:
- "I remember feeling that way at your stage."
- "It's okay to doubt yourself — keep going."

The Leadership Validation Equation

Presence + Listening + Acknowledgment = Influence

Validation isn't manipulation. It's leadership by relationship — not by control.

Studies in organizational psychology show that employees who feel validated by leadership demonstrate higher job satisfaction, lower burnout, and greater innovation (Edmondson, 1999; Goleman, 2006).

Reader:

So, if I want to be a validating leader, where do I start?

Dr. Sidor:

You start by making space before solutions. Don't rush to fix. First, reflect what you see or hear. That alone shifts power from dominance to dignity.

Dr. Dubin:

And you model it vertically and horizontally. You validate your team and yourself. You model it for peers and subordinates. Over time, validation becomes part of the culture – spoken and unspoken.

Reflections and Prompts

- Who modeled validation for you growing up or in your work life? What impact did it have?
- Where in your life are you a "leader" (formal or informal)? How might validation shift your influence?
- What would a validating version of your leadership voice sound like?

Practical Exercise

Validation Audit at Work or Home

For one day, notice how often you:

- Reflect back someone's feelings
- Validate before redirecting
- Create space before giving advice or direction

Then ask yourself:

- What changed in the tone of your interactions?
- What was the emotional impact on others?

Repeat weekly. Share results with someone close to you or a team member.

Chapter 12: Modeling Validation – At Work, Home, and in Leadership

Validation in Action – Home, Work, and Leadership

- Home: "I can see that you're having a hard time. Let's talk about it."
- Work: "I appreciate the effort you put into this project."
- Leadership: "It makes sense this is challenging — thank you for your honesty."

Validation strengthens relationships in every environment when it's modeled consistently.

Chart: Leadership Styles Comparison

COMMON LEADERSHIP STYLES VS. VALIDATION-BASED LEADERSHIP

COMMON LEADERSHIP STYLES			VALIDATION-BASED LEADERSHIP
1. AUTHORITARIAN	2. LAISSEZ-FAIRE	3. TRANSACTIONAL	ENCOURAGES AND SUPPORTS
RULES BY COMMAND	HANDS-OFF APPROACH	FOCUSES ON EXCHANGE	

Diagram: The Culture of Safety Model

Core: Validation → Builds Trust → Fosters Psychological Safety → Increases Engagement → Improves Outcomes

Validation is the core that enables open communication, belonging, and long-term retention in teams and families.

Table: Validating Language for Leaders and Caregivers

VALIDATING LANGUAGE	INVALIDATING LANGUAGE
I hear you.	That's not a big deal.
Help me understand your perspective.	You shouldn't feel that way.
What do you need to feel supported?	Just get over it.
Your feelings are valid.	Don't be so sensitive.
It's okay to feel that way.	Stop worrying about it.
I value your thoughts on this.	You don't know what you're talking about.
I appreciate your effort.	You could've done better.
I believe in your abilities.	You're not capable of that.
Your contribution matters.	Why are you even here?
It's normal to struggle; I'm here for you.	Everyone has problems, just deal with it.

Scientific References

- Edmondson, A. (1999). Psychological safety and learning behavior in work teams. Administrative Science Quarterly, 44(2), 350–383.
- Goleman, D. (2006). Social Intelligence: The New Science of Human Relationships. Bantam Books.
- Brown, B. (2018). Dare to Lead: Brave Work. Tough Conversations. Whole Hearts. Random House.
- Rogers, C. R. (1959). A theory of therapy, personality and interpersonal relationships. In Psychology: A Study of a Science, Vol. 3.

Chapter 13: Validation in Therapy, Teaching, Parenting, and Healing

Scene: A classroom, a therapy office, a home, a hospital bedside. Reader walks with Dr. Sidor and Dr. Dubin through each setting. In each, they witness something that either heals or harms — not the words, but the way they're offered.

Reader:

Everywhere I go now, I see it — places where validation is given, and places where it's missing. It's like I've been handed a new pair of glasses.

Dr. Dubin:

That's exactly it. Validation is the lens of healing. Whether you're sitting with a student, a child, a client, or a patient — before you educate, advise, or treat, you must first say, in some form: I see you.

Dr. Sidor:

This is true across every healing profession; and the science backs it up.

In therapy, validation increases emotional regulation and trust.

In education, it improves learning outcomes.

In parenting, it supports emotional development.

In medicine, it improves adherence and even physical health outcomes.

In Therapy:

Validation is the foundation of rapport and change.

DBT, ACT, psychodynamic therapy, and even CBT use some form of:

- "Your response makes sense given your history."
- "That's a natural way to feel in this situation."

Validation reduces defensiveness and increases client engagement (Linehan, 1993; Gilbert, 2009).

In Teaching:

Students need to feel seen before they can safely struggle.

- "That's a great question."
- "It's okay to not get it yet."
- "You're not alone in this."

Validation improves motivation, decreases shame, and supports cognitive flexibility (Deci & Ryan, 2000).

In Parenting:

A child's nervous system is shaped by how caregivers respond to their feelings.

- "It's okay to feel sad."
- "I hear that this is frustrating. I'm here with you."
- "Your emotions are welcome here."

Secure attachment is built on emotional validation, not just physical care (Siegel & Bryson, 2011).

In Healthcare and Healing Professions:

Whether you're a nurse, doctor, doula, or healer—your words shape trust.

- "I can see how that pain has affected your life."
- "You've been through a lot, and it's okay to feel overwhelmed."
- "You're not just a diagnosis—you're a whole person."

Studies show that patient satisfaction and recovery improve when providers validate emotional experience (Fogarty et al., 1999).

Reader:

So, before skill, before knowledge, before credentials — comes connection.

Dr. Sidor:

Exactly. Validation is what makes everything else land. It's not extra. It's essential.

Dr. Dubin:

It doesn't take more time. It takes more presence.

Reflections and Prompts

- When have you received validation in a professional or caregiving role? How did it affect you?
- In what moments have you skipped validation in your work or relationships—and what was the result?
- What's one phrase of validation you can start practicing in your role today?

Practical Exercise

Role-Based Validation Prompts

Choose your role(s) and pick one prompt to use daily this week:

- Therapist: "Given everything you've been through, your response makes sense."
- Teacher: "Your confusion is part of learning — thank you for being brave enough to ask."
- Parent: "I know this is hard. And I love you, no matter what."
- Healer/Provider: "You're more than what's wrong. You're everything that's still working too."

Journal what you noticed afterward. Did the energy shift?

Chapter 13: Validation in Therapy, Teaching, Parenting, and Healing

Chart: Validation Across Roles

VALIDATION ACROSS ROLES

ROLE	PHRASE	IMPACT	OUTCOME
Caregiver	"I'm here with you."	Comfort and support	Strengthening bond
Teacher	"Your effort shows."	Encouraging perseverancen	Stuctent engagement
Therapist	"That makes sense."	Affirming client's expene	Enhancing therapeuttic progress
Manager	"I value your input."	Recognizing employee's contributione	Boosting team morale

The Brain on Validation by Role

- **Therapy**: Activates ventral striatum (reward), prefrontal cortex (regulation)
- **Teaching**: Strengthens memory and motivation pathways (hippocampus, dopaminergic circuits)
- **Parenting**: Reduces amygdala reactivity, supports oxytocin release

Validation fosters emotional safety and neurobiological trust across roles.

The Healing Sequence

1. **Presence**: Show up and listen fully
2. **Validation**: Reflect and acknowledge the person's inner experience
3. **Safety**: Emotional and psychological calm arises
4. **Growth**: Self-trust, learning, and healing become possible

Table: Unintended vs. Intentional Validation

Unintended Invalidation	Intentional Validation
"It's not that bad."	"It makes sense you feel overwhelmed."
"You're being too sensitive."	"You're allowed to feel upset."
"Let's move on from this."	"This matters, and I want to honor it."
"You're fine."	"Tell me what's going on—I'm here."

Scientific References

- Linehan, M. M. (1993). Cognitive-Behavioral Treatment of Borderline Personality Disorder. Guilford Press.
- Gilbert, P. (2009). The Compassionate Mind. Constable & Robinson.
- Deci, E. L., & Ryan, R. M. (2000). Self-determination theory and the facilitation of intrinsic motivation, social development, and well-being. American Psychologist, 55(1), 68–78.
- Siegel, D. J., & Bryson, T. P. (2011). The Whole-Brain Child. Delacorte Press.
- Fogarty, L. A., et al. (1999). Patients' evaluations of the quality of pain management in hospitals. Journal of Pain and Symptom Management, 17(5), 333–340.

Chapter 14: The Art of Collective Validation – Cultures of Inclusion

Scene: A town hall gathering. Reader sits beside Dr. Dubin and Dr. Sidor in a circle of community leaders, educators, clinicians, parents, and residents. The topic: inclusion. The method: validation.

Reader:

I'm starting to see that validation doesn't just heal individuals or families – it has the power to shape entire systems. But how do we move from validating one person... to building a culture of validation?

Dr. Dubin:

By making validation a norm, not a luxury. It becomes the way we train, speak, write policy, hold meetings, and resolve conflict. It becomes part of the organizational nervous system.

Dr. Sidor:

And it starts with identity. Collective validation says: Your race, your gender, your story, your body, your background – they belong here. They matter.

Reader:

So, it's about justice, too?

Dr. Sidor:

Yes. Validation is a tool for equity and repair. Invalidation is at the root of oppression. Entire groups have been systemically told: "Your pain isn't real." "Your voice isn't welcome." "Your existence is inconvenient." Reversing that starts with: "We see you, we hear you, and you belong."

The Three Levels of Collective Validation

1. **Interpersonal Level** – The language we use with one another every day.
   "Thank you for sharing that—your experience is important."
2. **Institutional Level** – Policies, procedures, and practices that reflect dignity.
   Pronoun respect, trauma-informed supervision, inclusive decision-making.
3. **Cultural Level** – A shared ethos of honoring difference and listening deeply.
   Celebrating diverse narratives, de-centering dominant norms, and repairing harm with presence.

Practices That Build Inclusive Cultures Through Validation

- Begin meetings with acknowledgment of presence and emotion, not just agendas.
- Integrate lived experience into leadership and decision-making.
- Center stories of historically unseen groups—not as tokenism, but as truth.
- Replace "corrective" feedback with "connective" feedback.
- Make validation the first response in all conflict resolution protocols.

Research on inclusive leadership and psychological safety shows that validation enhances engagement, reduces turnover, and fosters innovation (Edmondson, 1999; Dovidio et al., 2002).

Dr. Dubin:

When validation becomes collective, we stop asking people to "earn" their place; rather, we build systems where people can be seen without shrinking and heard without harm.

Reader:

So, this is bigger than healing. It's how we rebuild the world.

Dr. Sidor:

Exactly. One conversation, one policy, one culture at a time.

Reflections and Prompts

- Where have you witnessed cultural or systemic invalidation?
- How might validation begin to shift that space?
- What's one practice you can bring into your team, classroom, or organization to foster inclusion?

Practical Exercise

The Collective Validation Circle

Gather your team or community group. Invite each person to complete this sentence aloud:

- "One part of my identity I've had to fight to have validated is…"
- "One thing I wish people knew or respected more is…"

Listen. Validate each other with reflective statements, not solutions.

This practice builds trust, equity, and connection.

Chapter 14: The Art of Collective Validation – Cultures of Inclusion

Infographic: The Three Levels of Collective Validation

Individual Level
Feeling seen, heard, and valued on a personal level.

Group Level
Acceptance and respect within a group or community.

Societal Level
Inclusivity and belonging in broader society.

This layered approach builds validation into the fabric of communities and systems.

From Invalidation to Inclusion

Invalidation ➜ Silence, exclusion, inequity

Validation ➜ Dialogue, belonging, empowerment

The shift begins when communities intentionally center validation at all levels.

Collective Validation Practices in Organizations

ORGANIZATIONAL PRACTICES
THAT SIGNAL COLLECTIVE VALIDATION

PRACTICE	SIGNAL
Open Communication	Transparency & Trust
Diverse Representation	Equity
Shared Decision-Making	Empowerment
Supportive Leadership	Psychological Safety

Table: Inclusive vs. Exclusive Language

Exclusive or Dismissive Language	Inclusive and Validating Language
"That's not a real issue."	"Your concerns are valid—let's explore them."
"We've always done it this way."	"How might we improve our practices to reflect everyone's needs?"
"This doesn't apply to you."	"We want this to feel relevant and inclusive to everyone."
"Some people just don't fit."	"We're stronger when we create space for diverse contributions."

Scientific References

- Edmondson, A. (1999). Psychological safety and learning behavior in work teams. Administrative Science Quarterly, 44(2), 350–383.
- Dovidio, J. F., Gaertner, S. L., & Saguy, T. (2009). Commonality and the complexity of "we": Social attitudes and identities in the United States and Israel. Social Issues and Policy Review, 3(1), 103–135.
- Sue, D. W., Capodilupo, C. M., et al. (2007). Racial microaggressions in everyday life: Implications for clinical practice. American Psychologist, 62(4), 271–286.
- Brown, B. (2018). Dare to Lead. Random House.

Here is Chapter 15 of *Before Anything Else, Validate* — the final chapter in the main body of the book. It brings everything full circle through the principle of reciprocity — showing that giving and receiving validation in balance is not just healing, it is wholeness.

Chapter 15: The Reciprocity Principle – Giving and Receiving in Balance

Scene: A sunlit garden. Reader walks side by side with Dr. Sidor and Dr. Dubin. The journey is almost complete, but one final insight emerges—a realization that validation is not just something we offer or seek. It's something we must also learn to receive.

Reader:

I've learned how to validate others.

I've learned how to validate myself.

But I still struggle when others try to validate me.

I deflect, dismiss, and downplay. Why is that?

Dr. Sidor:

Because receiving validation requires openness, safety, and self-trust. And if you've lived a life where validation was rare, conditional, or weaponized, receiving it can feel foreign — or even threatening.

Dr. Dubin:

Many of us learned to be caretakers, performers, and achievers. We give validation easily, but we don't believe we deserve it ourselves. Healing requires both: the humility to receive and the generosity to give.

The Reciprocity Principle: Four Truths

1. **Validation is a circle, not a hierarchy.**
   You're not "better" for giving it or "weaker" for needing it.
2. **You can't fully give what you haven't learned to receive.**
   Genuine validation flows from embodiment, not performance.
3. **Giving without receiving leads to burnout.**
   Receiving is replenishment, not selfishness.
4. **Receiving deepens empathy.**
   When you allow others to care for you, you understand the power of your own presence.

Reader:

So how do I practice receiving?

Dr. Dubin:

Start small. When someone compliments you, instead of deflecting, say:

"Thank you. That means a lot." When someone validates your feelings, pause and breathe it in. Let it land.

Dr. Sidor:

And then reflect. Ask yourself:

- "What part of me struggled to accept that?"
- "What would it mean if it were true?"

This is how you build the muscle of receiving without resistance.

Giving, Receiving, and the Flow of Human Connection

Interaction	Without Validation	With Validation
Support	Feels transactional or empty	Feels nourishing and mutual
Leadership	Feels controlling or performative	Feels relational and trust-based
Intimacy	Feels unsafe or uncertain	Feels grounded and emotionally open
Friendship	Feels lopsided or exhausting	Feels reciprocal and energizing

Reflections and Prompts

- When someone validates you, what is your instinctive reaction—do you deflect, embrace, or doubt it?
- Who in your life offers you sincere validation? How do you respond to them?
- What belief might you need to unlearn in order to receive with grace?

Practical Exercise

The Receiving Challenge

For the next 3 days:

- Say "thank you" without a qualifier when someone validates you.
- Write down how it felt.
- Reflect: What did you notice in your body? What emotions came up?

This challenge helps retrain your nervous system to accept worth without resistance.

Chapter 15: The Reciprocity Principle – Giving and Receiving in Balance

Infographic: The Reciprocity Loop

1. Give validation to others → Builds connection
2. Others feel seen → Offer validation in return
3. You feel supported → Trust increases
4. Internal self-worth grows → Repeat the cycle

This loop shows how balanced relationships nurture mutual validation and well-being.

Table: Resistance to Receiving Validation

Common Resistance Response	Reframe or Self-Validation Response
"It wasn't a big deal."	"Thank you. That means a lot to me."
"I got lucky."	"I worked hard and I'm proud of it."
"You don't have to say that."	"It feels good to be seen."
"I should have done more."	"I did my best and that's enough today."

Diagram: The Circle of Mutual Worth

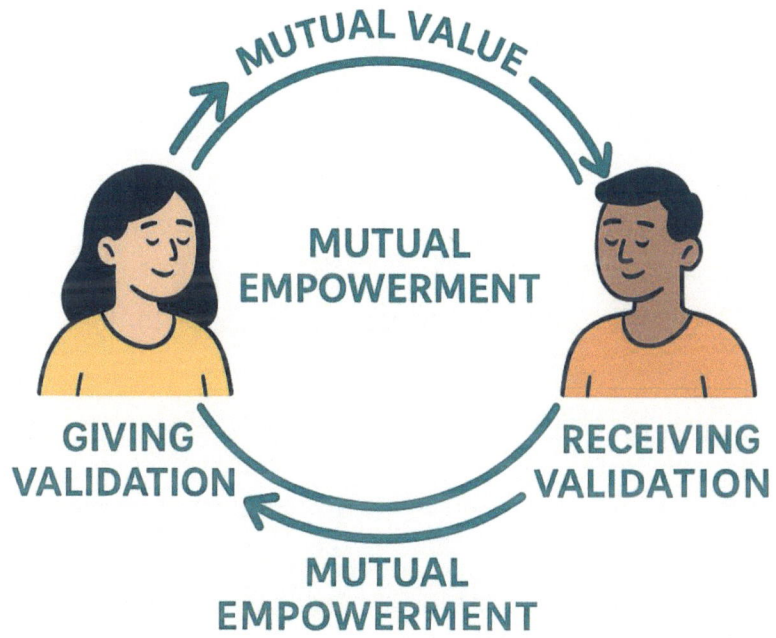

This circular model emphasizes that giving and receiving validation are interdependent parts of thriving connection.

Checklist: Are You Open to Receiving?

Are You Open to Receiving?

- [ ] I accept compliments and praise without deflecting or minimizing.
- [ ] I say "thank you" when someone offers me validation or support.
- [ ] I allow myself to be helped and supported by others.
- [ ] I believe I am worthy of receiving kindness, appreciation, and care.
- [ ] I feel comfortable experiencing positive emotions like joy or pride.
- [ ] I recognize that accepting validation is not selfish or weak.
- [ ] I practice self-compassion and recognize my own progress.
- [ ] I welcome constructive feedback and use it for growth.
- [ ] I listen to others' expressions of gratitude or appreciation for me.
- [ ] I acknowledge my achievements and validate my efforts

Scientific References

- Neff, K. D. (2003). Self-compassion: An alternative conceptualization of a healthy attitude toward oneself. Self and Identity, 2(2), 85–101.
- Brown, B. (2010). The Gifts of Imperfection. Hazelden Publishing.
- Gergen, K. J. (2009). Relational Being: Beyond Self and Community. Oxford University Press.
- Miller, J. B. (1986). Toward a New Psychology of Women. Beacon Press.

Epilogue: You Were Always Enough

There is a quiet truth that sits at the center of every human being.

It does not shout. It does not compete. It does not seek approval, performance, or perfection.

It simply waits — for you to come home to it.

You were always enough.

Before the gold stars and the report cards.

Before the broken mirrors and missing apologies.

Before the identity you performed and the love you tried to earn.

Before the striving, the proving, the pleasing.

Before the first wound and after the last mistake —

You were enough.

Validation, real validation, isn't something we find. It's something we remember.

It was there in your first breath. It will still be there in your last.

This book is not just a guide — it is a mirror, a map, a movement.

And it ends where all true healing begins:

Not with fixing. Not with becoming.

But with seeing. With honoring. With returning.

To the truth that never stopped being true:

You are valid. You are worthy. You are enough.

Conclusion: The New Way Forward

If you've made it this far, something has already shifted in you.

You've seen how validation is not just a tool or a technique—it is a truth, a need, and a power. You've uncovered the patterns of seeking and suppression, the hidden pain of being unseen, and the quiet strength of self-recognition.

You've also learned that validation isn't a one-time act—it's a way of being.

A way of listening before reacting.

A way of seeing before solving.

A way of honoring before advising.

A way of holding space for humanity—yours and others.

And now, it's time to bring this into the world.

Because someone will walk into your office today who just wants to know they're not crazy.

A child will melt down, not for attention—but for connection.

A friend will go silent, waiting to see if their story is too much.

A colleague will falter, unsure if they belong at the table.

And your presence—anchored in validation—can change everything.

You don't have to be perfect.

You don't have to say all the right words.

But if you can pause, breathe, and see them—you've already begun the work.

This is how healing spreads.

This is how cultures shift.

This is how we build a world where no one has to fight to be seen.

So here's the challenge, the invitation, the mission:

Before anything else, validate.

Start there. Stay there. Lead from there.

And watch what unfolds.

Invitation to the Reader

Dear Reader,

You've taken a bold and tender journey—one that began not with doing, but with seeing—Seeing yourself, seeing others, seeing the quiet power of validation as the language of healing, connection, and transformation.

This book was never meant to be just a book. It's a mirror, a movement, a new way of being. And now, it's yours.

We invite you to pause here and ask yourself:

- What has shifted in how you see yourself?
- What have you begun to forgive, to acknowledge, or to allow?
- Who might be waiting for your presence, your pause, your validation?

Please don't stop here.

Practice what you've learned, share the tools, and teach it forward.

Use the language of validation in your homes, your teams, your classrooms, your therapy sessions, your communities.

You don't need a title to lead—only presence and intention.

And if this book has spoken to you, helped you feel more whole, or offered something meaningful in your life—we'd be honored if you left a review. Your voice helps others find their way to these pages, too. And in doing so, you help validate this mission.

Let this be more than a book. Let it be the start of something real.

Before anything else, validate.

Always.

With appreciation,

The Authors
Mardoche Sidor, M.D.
Karen Dubin, Ph.D., LCSW
SWEET Institute

Final Acknowledgments

This book was written in devotion—to healing, to wholeness, to the possibility that every human being might one day feel fully seen.

To everyone who held space for this project while it was still an unspoken longing—thank you.

To those who reminded us to rest, reflect, and return to what matters—your presence made this possible.

To the communities that continue to teach us the true meaning of resilience, connection, and dignity—you are the soul of this work.

We thank every reader who shows up not only for others, but for themselves. You are proof that inner work is world work.

To the clinicians and caregivers, educators and leaders, parents and peers—thank you for choosing validation as a daily act of courage. You are helping create a world where people feel safe to speak, safe to feel, safe to be.

To those whose stories will never make it into textbooks, but live in every act of survival, kindness, and truth—you are our greatest inspiration.

And finally, to the parts of ourselves we once ignored, silenced, or misunderstood—thank you for waiting.

This book is our offering. May it ripple far beyond us.

With deepest gratitude,

Mardoche Sidor, M.D.
Karen Dubin, Ph.D., LCSW
SWEET Institute

Reader Integration Toolkit

Turning Insight into Action — Daily, Practically, Sustainably

You've read the stories. You've seen the science. You've felt the call.

Now it's time to live it.

This toolkit is designed to help you apply the message of *Before Anything Else, Validate* in real life. Whether you're a clinician, educator, parent, leader, or lifelong learner — these tools will help you practice validation as a lifestyle, not just a concept.

1. The Daily Validation Pause (30 seconds)

Use this anytime emotions rise — in yourself or someone else.

Step 1: Pause. Take a breath.

Step 2: Ask, "What is being felt right now?"

Step 3: Reflect it back — "It makes sense."

Step 4: Choose compassion before action.

Practice this at home, work, in conflict, or in silence with yourself.

2. The 3-Part Self-Validation Script

Use this when your inner critic gets loud.

"This is how I feel…"

"It makes sense because…"

"And I choose to respond with kindness."

Use it in writing, out loud, or in front of a mirror.

3. The Weekly Integration Journal

Once a week, ask yourself:

- When did I validate myself this week?
- When did I invalidate myself — and what could I say differently next time?
- Who did I validate?
- What opportunity to validate someone did I miss?
- What does my nervous system need more of this week — safety, rest, acknowledgment?

4. Validation Scripts for Everyday Life

Situation	Validation Response
Someone is upset	"That sounds really hard."
You made a mistake	"I'm learning. It's okay to be human."
A child is crying	"You're allowed to feel this. I'm here."
A coworker speaks up	"Thank you for sharing that — it's important."
You feel overwhelmed	"Of course this feels like a lot. I've got me."

5. The Integration Commitment

Choose one:

- I will pause before I react.
- I will validate myself at least once per day.
- I will start one conversation each day with acknowledgment.
- I will challenge my internal critic with compassion.
- I will model validation in one meeting, session, or meal this week.

6. The Ripple Tracker

Every time you validate someone this week, write it down.

"I saw them... I said... I noticed..."

Reflect at the end of the week:

Did anything shift—in them, in me, in us?

Remember:

Validation is not about having the perfect words. It's about presence before problem-solving, compassion before correction, and truth before technique.

Before anything else, validate.

Appendices and Tools

Appendix A: Daily Self-Validation Tracker

Instructions: Use this daily to strengthen the habit of validating yourself.

Day	I Validated Myself By...	What I Felt After	Notes or Reflections
1			
2			
3			

Appendix B: The 3-Step Self-Validation Script

1. Acknowledge – "I feel ___. This is what's happening for me."
2. Normalize – "It makes sense I feel this way because ___."
3. Compassionate Response – "I'm here for me. I'm doing my best."

Appendix C: Validation vs. Invalidation Language Guide

Situation	Invalidating Response	Validating Response
Someone is upset	"Calm down."	"It makes sense you're upset."
A child is crying	"Don't cry, you're fine."	"I can see you're hurting. I'm here."
In conflict	"You're overreacting."	"I hear that this really affected you."

Appendix D: 21-Day Validation Practice Calendar

Day	Practice	Reflection Prompt
1	Mirror work (2 minutes)	"What was hard or healing about this?"
2	Validate someone at work	"How did they respond?"
3	Journal about a time you felt unseen	"What did you need then?"
...	...	...

Appendix E: Group Exercise – The Validation Circle

Instructions: In a circle, invite each person to complete:

- "One thing I wish people knew about me is…"

Others respond with reflective, nonjudgmental statements:

- "That makes sense."
- "Thank you for sharing."
- "I hear you."

Appendix F: Validation in Leadership Checklist

- I pause before responding.
- I reflect feelings before offering advice.
- I create safety for disagreement.
- I affirm effort as well as outcome.
- I model validation up, down, and across.

Appendix G: Self-Validation Journal Prompts

Use these for morning reflection or evening integration:

- "Today I felt ___, and it makes sense because ___."
- "A part of me is afraid that ___. I want to tell that part…"
- "The version of me I'm becoming believes…"
- "If I fully validated myself today, I would…"

Appendix H: Printable Affirmation Cards (suggested content)
You may print or cut out these cards to keep in your wallet, desk, or mirror:

- "My feelings make sense."
- "I don't need to earn my worth."
- "I am safe with myself."
- "I can hold space for others without abandoning myself."
- "I am allowed to rest, to be, to feel."

Scientific Reference List

Validation & Emotional Regulation:

- Linehan, M. M. (1993). Cognitive-Behavioral Treatment of Borderline Personality Disorder. Guilford Press.
- Neff, K. D. (2003). Self-compassion: An alternative conceptualization of a healthy attitude toward oneself. Self and Identity, 2(2), 85–101.
- Gilbert, P. (2009). The Compassionate Mind. Constable & Robinson.
- Goldin, P. R., et al. (2009). The neural bases of emotion regulation. Biological Psychiatry, 65(5), 367–373.

Neuroscience & Self-Worth:

- Cascio, C. N., et al. (2016). Self-affirmation activates the ventral striatum. Psychological Science, 27(4), 455–466.
- Siegel, D. J. (2010). The Mindful Therapist. Norton.
- Creswell, J. D., et al. (2013). Neural reactivity to emotional stimuli and resilience. Emotion, 13(5), 1091–1098.

Attachment & Development:

- Ainsworth, M. D. S. (1979). Infant–mother attachment. American Psychologist, 34(10), 932–937.
- Bowlby, J. (1988). A Secure Base: Parent-Child Attachment and Healthy Human Development. Basic Books.
- Siegel, D. J., & Bryson, T. P. (2011). The Whole-Brain Child. Delacorte Press.

Self-Compassion & Internal Dialogue:

- Neff, K. D., & Germer, C. K. (2013). The Mindful Self-Compassion program. Journal of Clinical Psychology, 69(1), 28–44.
- Schwartz, R. C. (2001). Internal Family Systems Therapy. Guilford Press.
- Young, J. E., Klosko, J. S., & Weishaar, M. E. (2003). Schema Therapy: A Practitioner's Guide. Guilford Press.

Organizational Psychology & Validation in Leadership:

- Edmondson, A. (1999). Psychological safety and learning behavior in work teams. Administrative Science Quarterly, 44(2), 350–383.
- Goleman, D. (2006). Social Intelligence: The New Science of Human Relationships. Bantam.
- Brown, B. (2018). Dare to Lead. Random House.
- Dovidio, J. F., Gaertner, S. L., & Saguy, T. (2009). Social attitudes and identities. Social Issues and Policy Review, 3(1), 103–135.

Recommended Reading

Expand Your Journey — Books That Deepen, Affirm, and Sustain the Work

On Self-Compassion and Inner Dialogue
- Self-Compassion by Kristin Neff
- The Mindful Self-Compassion Workbook by Kristin Neff & Christopher Germer
- Radical Acceptance by Tara Brach
- The Gifts of Imperfection by Brené Brown
- Loving What Is by Byron Katie

On Validation and Emotional Safety
- Cognitive-Behavioral Treatment of Borderline Personality Disorder by Marsha Linehan
- The Whole-Brain Child by Daniel J. Siegel & Tina Payne Bryson
- The Language of Emotions by Karla McLaren
- Nonviolent Communication by Marshall B. Rosenberg
- What Happened to You? by Bruce D. Perry & Oprah Winfrey

On Neuroscience and the Brain
- The Mindful Brain by Daniel J. Siegel
- The Body Keeps the Score by Bessel van der Kolk
- Hardwiring Happiness by Rick Hanson
- The Polyvagal Theory by Stephen W. Porges

On Trauma, Identity, and Belonging
- My Grandmother's Hands by Resmaa Menakem
- You Are the One You've Been Waiting For by Richard Schwartz
- Homecoming by John Bradshaw
- The Drama of the Gifted Child by Alice Miller
- Permission to Feel by Marc Brackett

On Leadership and Culture Change
- Dare to Lead by Brené Brown
- The Fearless Organization by Amy C. Edmondson
- Start With Why by Simon Sinek
- The 7 Habits of Highly Effective People by Stephen R. Covey

On Healing, Growth, and the Human Spirit
- When the Body Says No by Gabor Maté
- The Art of Possibility by Rosamund Stone Zander & Benjamin Zander
- Man's Search for Meaning by Viktor E. Frankl
- Let Your Life Speak by Parker J. Palmer
- The Untethered Soul by Michael A. Singer

More from SWEET Institute Publishing

Transformational Books for a Transformational World

At SWEET Institute Publishing, we believe in writing books that don't just inform—but transform. Our titles are written by clinicians, teachers, healers, and visionaries who are committed to helping people move from knowledge to implementation, from intellectual understanding to lived experience.

If you found *Before Anything Else, Validate* meaningful, you may also enjoy:

The Kindness Imperative (In Print)

How Power Becomes Purpose, and Why True Greatness Begins with Grace

A powerful exploration of kindness as the hidden force behind true leadership, lasting impact, and emotional well-being.

The Simplicity Principle (In Print)

How Breaking Things Down Can Help You Learn Faster, Heal Deeper, and Live Freely

A revolutionary look at how simplifying thoughts, behaviors, and systems leads to clarity, confidence, and change.

Before Anything Else, Breathe (In Print)

A Guide to Reclaiming Presence, Peace, and Self-Regulation Through Breath Awareness

Practical, science-backed guidance on how to use your breath as a tool for healing, grounding, and transformation.

How Life Works (In Print)

A Journey Through Patterns, Purpose, and the Lessons We Keep Repeating

A story-driven, science-informed guide to the life lessons that shape us—and how to consciously learn them for good.

The Courage to Care

Stories of Healing, Hope, and the Power of Social Work

A collection of real stories from frontline clinicians that affirms the heart of the helping professions.

I Didn't Say Enough (In Print)

How the Unspoken Shapes Us—And How to Speak the Truth That Heals

A brave invitation to reclaim your voice, confront internalized silence, and speak truth in a world that needs it.

―――

Stay Connected

Explore our growing library at SweetInstitutePublishing.com

Join our newsletter for book releases, author events, and exclusive tools.

Follow us on social media @SWEETInstitute

Let's change the world—one insight, one page, one person at a time.

About the Authors

Mardoche Sidor, M.D.

Dr. Mardoche Sidor is a Harvard and Columbia-trained quadruple board-certified psychiatrist (General Psychiatry, Child and Adolescent Psychiatry, Forensic Psychiatry, and Addiction Psychiatry) with additional training in Geriatric and Public/Community Psychiatry. He has served as Assistant Clinical Professor of Psychiatry at Columbia University and is the current Medical Director of Urban Pathways, where he leads system-wide clinical transformation initiatives.

Dr. Sidor is the co-founder of the SWEET Institute, where he has pioneered evidence-based, dignity-centered models of care for clinicians, social service professionals, and the people they serve. He is known for his ability to bridge clinical science with human-centered healing. Through his teaching, writing, and leadership, he has helped thousands transform their lives and their work.

Karen Dubin, Ph.D., LCSW

Dr. Karen Dubin is a licensed clinical social worker, trauma-informed educator, and co-founder of the SWEET Institute. She holds a Ph.D. in Social Work with a specialization in relational and behavioral change. Her work centers on the intersection of neuroscience, emotional intelligence, and the power of presence in healing.

With a background in both clinical practice and higher education, Dr. Dubin brings a rare combination of academic rigor and therapeutic depth. She is a master facilitator, writer, and curriculum designer, known for helping individuals and organizations transform how they show up—for themselves, for others, and for the world.

SWEET Institute

Founded by Dr. Sidor and Dr. Dubin, the SWEET Institute (Supporting Wellbeing Through Empowerment, Education, and Training) is an international organization dedicated to rehumanizing care, redefining leadership, and reimagining mental health from the inside out.

With a global network of clinicians, caregivers, educators, and changemakers, SWEET provides cutting-edge learning experiences, community-driven transformation, and a publishing platform for voices that heal.

Learn more at: www.SWEETInstitute.com

www.ingramcontent.com/pod-product-compliance
Lightning Source LLC
Chambersburg PA
CBHW042320150426
43192CB00001B/4